COOKING GAME:

BEST WILD GAME RECIPES
FROM THE READERS OF
DEER & DEER HUNTING

Published by

Krause Publications a division of F+W Media, Inc.
700 East State Street • Iola, WI 54990-0001
715-445-2214 • 888-457-2873
www.krausebooks.com

To order books or other products call toll-free 1-800-258-0929
or visit us online at www.shopdeerhunting.com

ISBN-13: 978-1-4402-3513-9
ISBN-10: 1-4402-3513-9

Cover Design by Dustin Reid
Designed by Sandi Carpenter
Edited by Jacob Edson

Printed in the United States of America

About This Book

You've filled your tag or hit your limit. The wild game is field dressed, packaged, froze and ready to prepare for the dinner table. The hard work is done, and it's finally time to enjoy the spoils of your hunt.

But what should you make? The options are endless. That's where this book comes in. We've collected some of our readers' most loved recipes in an attempt to help you prepare the most delicious wild game possible. These are family favorites that you can prepare in your own kitchen without having to be an expert chef. The collection of mouth-watering recipes comes from all regions of the country and covers everything from doves and turkeys to deer and gators.

The folks that submitted these dishes live and breathe the outdoors. They know how to wow friends and family with delicious wild game. So, set the table and get ready to try something new and exciting.

Contents

Introduction

Handling Game

Tasty game results from proper handling from the moment you kill it to the time you place the packaged cuts in the freezer. Proper care includes field dressing, cooling, skinning, storage and butchering.

Step 1: Field Dressing
Field dressing is an extremely important step in the handling of game. Removing the paunch, intestines and other inedible internal tissue permits body heat to dissipate quickly, thus cooling the meat. This step remains important in either warm or cool weather.
Equally important, field dressing eliminates the possibility of stomach acids and expanding gases tainting the meat. It also helps to completely drain blood from the body cavity.
Although many novice hunters think that field dressing requires special skills, it's not really a complicated task.

Step 2: Cooling
Whether you immediately transport your game home or leave it in camp, the animal should be hung as soon as possible. Hanging game accomplishes two things: it facilitates cooling, and it puts the animal in a good position for skinning. Propping the body cavity open with a stick promotes even faster cooling. Many people hang large game head up, but a head down position remains better for several reasons. First, it allows heat to rise freely from the chest cavity. Second, it makes it easier to skin the animal. Third, it reduces the amount of hair you get on the meat.
Select a shady, cool spot for hanging. If temperatures stay at or below 40 to 50 degrees, the meat will stay in good condition for two or three days. Obviously, during late fall in Northern states, game could hang longer without undesirable effect on the meat.

In Southern states, however, and during early seasons around the country, hot daytime temperatures present a problem. The warmer the weather, the sooner the meat should be processed. Hanging game in a walk-in cooler is ideal, but not all hunting camps have one. In that case, quarter large game and put the meat on ice.

Step 3: Skinning
In cool climates, wait to skin the animal. Skinning game accelerates cooling of the meat, and skinning is easiest when the carcass is still warm. However, the skin helps protect the meat from the elements while it is hanging. It also prevents the meat from drying out.

In extremely cold weather, leaving the hide on the carcass can help prevent the meat from freezing unevenly. Meat quality depends upon rapid, but uniform cooling. Quick freezing, or repeated freezing and thawing, can cause meat to be tough.

In warm regions, skin large game as soon as possible. This will help the meat cool faster. If the game is to be hung in a cooler, the hide will not be needed for protection.

If you do not immediately butcher the skinned game carcass, cover the meat with a white, commercial cheesecloth. Such game bags permit further cooling and air circulation, while also keeping out insects. You can discourage flies from attacking the exposed meat by liberally sprinkling black pepper on it.

Step 4: Aging
The question of whether one should age meat or not remains a point of endless discussion among hunters, meat processors and scientists alike.

Some animal scientists view aging as impractical because so many people lack the proper facilities. Under improper conditions, the meat becomes susceptible to deterioration by bacteria and mold growth. Further, since hunters shoot a large number of young animals with naturally tender meat, aging seems unnecessary. However, holding the carcass at temperatures of 34 to 37 degrees Fahrenheit with a relative humidity of 88 percent allows the enzymes in the meat to break down some of the complex proteins, a process that usually improves flavor and tenderness.

Step 5: Butchering
In the absence of experience or a willing instructor, most hunters take large game to a local processor to have it butchered, for a fee. In most cases, however, even the novice ends up with better quality venison when he butchers his animal himself.

Surprisingly, it takes very little practice to become proficient at butchering game, and you don't need any special tools other than a sharp, stiff knife and a steel to keep it sharp. As a side benefit, the butchering process also offers an opportunity for you to become familiar with animal physiology. This knowledge naturally translates into better understanding of shot placement.

Chapter 1

Venison Appetizers

Stuffed Peppers

Robert Vaillancourt, NH   *Serves 4, or in my home 2*

1 pound ground venison
1 medium onion, diced
1 package saltine crackers, crushed
2 eggs

Salt and pepper to taste
4 medium peppers
1/4-inch cheese cubes, any flavor
Ketchup

In a mixing bowl, thoroughly mix the ground venison, onion, crackers, eggs, salt and pepper. Clean out the peppers and stuff them with the meat mixture. Top stuffed peppers with ketchup and place in baking dish small enough to hold them from falling over. Bake at 350° for 15 to 20 minutes. Turn heat down to 250°, top stuffed peppers with the cheese cubes and continue to bake for 10 minutes or until cheese is melted. Remove from oven and let stand to cool slightly before serving.

Spicy Venison Meatballs

Scott O'Brien, OH

1 pound ground venison
1 pound hot and spicy sausage
3 cups bread crumbs

3 eggs
2 large jars spaghetti sauce
Olive or vegetable oil

In a large mixing bowl, thoroughly mix the sausage and venison together. Then mix in the eggs and bread crumbs. Roll into bite-size balls, 1-inch to 1-1/2-inches. In a frying pan on medium heat, add enough oil to keep the balls from sticking. Cook the meatballs long enough to brown the outside. Once browned, drain any excess oil or grease, and place the meatballs and spaghetti sauce into a crock pot. Cook the meatballs on high for 2 hours turning the meatballs every 30 minutes. Turn crock pot to low, cook for 30 minutes and serve.

Apple-Venison Meatballs

Christopher Tarter, KY

1 pound ground venison
1 large apple
2 tablespoons dehydrated minced onion
1/2 teaspoon salt
Fresh ground pepper to taste

1/3 cup seasoned dry bread crumbs
1 cup dry red wine
One 8-ounce can tomato sauce
1 teaspoon sugar
1 teaspoon dried rosemary
2 tablespoons olive oil

Combine venison with apple, onion, salt and pepper into large mixing bowl. Shape meatballs about 1-inch diameter. Roll in bread crumbs to coat. In a 4 cup measure, combine wine, tomato sauce, sugar and rosemary. Set aside.

In 12-inch nonstick skillet, heat oil over medium heat add meatballs, cook 5 to 7 minutes or until browned. Pour wine mixture over meatballs. Reduce heat to medium-low. Cover and simmer for 10 minutes. Serve over a bed of egg noodles.

Venison Taco Dip

This is great as a quick and easy appetizer when folks drop by unexpectedly, or as a single dish, stand-alone meal. —Dave Sien, MD

1 pound ground venison
1 package taco seasoning
1 large bag of tortilla chips

1 cup sour cream
1 jar queso cheese dip
16-ounce jar of salsa
Sliced jalapeños (optional)

Brown venison in a skillet, adding the taco seasoning and water per the packet's directions. (If frozen, can toss meat in skillet, and break up pretty quickly over low heat).

Place the tortilla chips in a large serving bowl. Top with the meat and the jar of queso cheese dip (heated in the microwave). Top with sour cream and salsa. Use surrounding chips to dip and eat!

Venison Wellington Rolls

Dan Barker, WI

1 pound venison ground or cubed into small pieces (lately I've been using ground Italian venison)
1 large package mushrooms, chopped small
1 small to medium sweet onion, chopped small
Garlic, salt, pepper and any other seasoning you like
Shredded cheese (4 cheese Mexican or what you like)
1 package puff pastry dough, thawed
2 eggs, beaten

In a large frying pan add some butter and olive oil on medium-high heat. Add venison and let sear; add in onions, mushroom and seasonings. Cook on medium-high heat until mushrooms are cooked down and starting to brown. Remove and cool mixture.

On counter-top, spread some flour and unfold puff pastry dough. Cut at the seams so you have 3 pieces that are about 3-inch by 10-inch. Spoon the cooled mixture onto center of pastry, creating a 3/4-inch to 1-inch row. Sprinkle with shredded cheese. Fold lower edge over mixture and roll into a tube. Place on cookie sheet lined with parchment paper, repeat with all 6 rolls.

Cut rolls into 1-inch to 1-1/2-inch sections then score the top of each piece with a 45-degree angle. Brush top with beaten egg mixture. Bake at 350° for 20 to 30 minutes or until pastry is golden brown. Before removing from sheet, re-cut the sections, place on serving tray and enjoy.

Deer Dip

Neal Fuquea, GA

1 pound deer burger
16-ounce sour cream
8-ounce cream cheese
1 package taco seasoning

1 package shredded cheese
2 cans black olives, chopped or sliced
1 tomato, chopped
1 bag tortilla chips

Brown meat in a skillet, set aside. In a mixing bowl, mix together sour cream, cream cheese and taco seasoning. Add browned meat and sprinkle with the remaining ingredients.

Perfect Venison Appetizers

Frank Farr, IL

Venison, cut in strips
1 small jar apricot preserves
1 half pint good bourbon
Salt and pepper to taste

1 bunch green onion
Green peppers, sliced thinly
Portobello mushrooms
Bacon

Marinate venison in preserves and bourbon overnight. Wrap venison strips, green onion, pepper and mushrooms with a strip of bacon and grill for 3 to 4 minutes. Perfect appetizer, also good made with duck breasts.

Bacon Venison Appetizers

Doug Aarons, MS

1/2 pound venison tenderloin
3 tablespoons zesty Italian dressing
12 bacon slices

1/4 cup cream cheese
12 slices pickled jalapeño peppers
1/2 teaspoon seasoning salt (or to taste)

Cut the venison tenderloin into 12 strips lengthwise. Toss with Italian dressing, and allow to marinate for 1 hour in the refrigerator.

Preheat a grill for medium heat.

Assemble the venison wraps, lay a strip of venison on top of a strip of bacon. Place one teaspoon of cream cheese at one end, and top with a slice of jalapeño. Roll up and secure with a skewer. Repeat with remaining ingredients. Season the wraps with desired amount of seasoning salt.

Grill for about 10 to 12 minutes, then turn over, and continue cooking until the bacon is crisp. Enjoy with beer and football!

Sweet Bacon-Wrapped Venison Tenderloin

Luell Bill, TX

2 pounds venison tenderloin
1/2 pound bacon (plain, thin-sliced bacon is best)
3 cups dark brown sugar
2 cups soy sauce (regular, NOT low-sodium. You'll want the saltiness)
1/4 cup white sugar (optional for added sweetness)

Mix brown sugar and soy sauce together in a bowl. They should combine nicely into a soupy soy liquid. Put tenderloin in a cooking tray. Pour soy sauce mixture over tenderloin. Roll tenderloin over in mixture, completely covering it. Let marinate at least 3 hours or overnight in refrigerator. It's best to marinate for 8 hours if you have the time. Also, it's GREAT to use a vacuum-seal device to seal the meat with the marinade. With this method, you can achieve overnight-level marinade in just a couple hours.

Remove tenderloin from tray, and place on a slotted bake sheet with a drip pan or aluminum foil below to catch dripping. Save the marinade.

Wrap a piece of bacon around the very end of the tenderloin, securing the bacon strip with a toothpick, repeating until the entire tenderloin is wrapped in 10 or so bacon "loops." The tenderloin should look like an arm with a bunch of wrist watches on it, the watches being the bacon strips.

Drizzle remaining marinade over tenderloin. Continue to baste with the marinade throughout the cooking process with either a brush or a turkey baster.

Place on center rack in oven and bake at 350° F for 30 to 40 minutes. This should cook the meat to about medium. For those of you who prefer rare meat (like me), cut the time to 25 to 30 minutes and then follow with the OPTION 2 step below regarding searing.

OPTION 1 - With about 10 minutes of cooking time left, you can lightly dust the top of the tenderloin with white sugar. This creates a sweet crust on top of the bacon. Might be too sweet for some. Try doing it on just HALF of the loin to see if you like it!

OPTION 2 - For a crispier crust and crispier bacon, remove tenderloin from oven and place directly on a grill over medium-high heat to sear the bacon and outer loin.

Remove from oven and place on cutting board. Using a knife, cut the loin between each strip of bacon so that you have many pieces of meat, each with their own toothpick.

Texas Venison

Jesus Armas Jr., FL

2 pounds venison steak	2 beef bouillon cubes
1-1/2 teaspoons Papa's Seasoned Salt	1/2 teaspoon dried Mexican oregano
1 cup all-purpose flour	1 bay leaf
4 tablespoons vegetable oil	2 dried red chile peppers
1/2 cup sliced onion	2 cups water
1/2 teaspoon ground cumin	

Lightly season the venison steaks with 1/2 teaspoon of Papa's Seasoning Salt. Cut the steaks into bite-sized pieces. Mix the flour with 1 teaspoon of Papa's salt; reserve 1 tablespoon of the flour mixture and set aside. Toss the cubed meat in the seasoned flour.

Heat the oil in the pressure cooker or a skillet over medium-high heat. Add the meat cubes in batches and cook until richly browned on all sides. Remove the meat and set aside.

Reduce the heat to medium, stir the reserved tablespoon of seasoned flour and the ground cumin into the pan drippings. Cook and stir until the flour has lost its raw smell and is lightly browned, about 5 minutes. Add the sliced onion and cook, stirring often, until the onion has softened, about 5 minutes.

Return the meat to the pan, along with the beef bouillon cubes, Mexican oregano, bay leaf, and chile peppers (remove the stems, but leave them whole). Pour in the water and seal the pressure cooker, turning the heat up to high.

Bring the pressure up to high and reduce the heat to maintain the pressure. Cook at high pressure for 15 minutes. Turn off the heat and let the pressure drop naturally. Remove the lid. Remove the chile peppers and bay leaf; squeeze the pulp from the peppers, returning the pulp to the pan and discarding the skins and the bay leaf. Taste and adjust the seasonings.

Deer Wings

Michael Donahue, NY

1-1/2 cups Worcestershire sauce
1-1/2 cups raspberry vinaigrette
2 pounds bacon
2 back straps

Toothpicks
2 cups Catalina dressing
Hot sauce of choice

In large bowl that has a tight lid, mix Worcestershire sauce and raspberry vinaigrette. Cut back straps into bite size pieces. Set aside in separate bowl. Wrap pieces in bacon and hold together with a toothpick. Usually 1 strip of bacon will wrap 3 pieces. Place wraps in marinade and marinate overnight. Two nights are even better.

Grill until bacon is done. You'll need to keep an eye on these babies and turn them often! If you have a side burner on the grill, pourπ into a skillet the Catalina dressing and hot sauce, to taste.

When "deer wings" are done move from grill to Catalina hot sauce pan and keep on low to keep warm, mixing them in the sauce mixture. Grab a toothpick and eat-em-up!

Mustard-Fried Venison

George Denka, SC

6 ounces venison cubes (per person)
1 jar yellow mustard
1 pound flour

1 jar cracked pepper
1 quart peanut oil

Cut venison into bite-sized cubes (I prefer to use cubed steak or backstrap). In a large bowl, mix mustard with cracked pepper (to your taste). Drag the venison cubes through the mustard and pepper mixture; then put into a gallon sized zip-lock bag or paper bag filled with flour. Shake until venison cubes are evenly covered with flour.

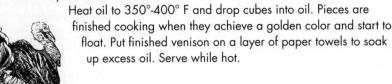

Heat oil to 350°-400° F and drop cubes into oil. Pieces are finished cooking when they achieve a golden color and start to float. Put finished venison on a layer of paper towels to soak up excess oil. Serve while hot.

Venison Poppers

Dan Morlock, MN

Rice wine vinegar	Venison steaks
Soy sauce	Jalapeños
Honey	Cheddar cheese
Pepper	

In a bowl, whisk the first 4 ingredients. Marinate the steaks overnight. Grill the steaks for about 4 minutes on each side. Cut up the steak and cheese into bite-size pieces. Slice the jalapeños (remove seeds if you do not want them super spicy).

Stack the steak, cheese and jalapeños with a toothpick.

Line them up on a baking sheet and bake at 350° F until the cheese melts.

Deer Poppers

Richard Smitherman, AL

6 large jalapeño peppers	1/2 pound cheddar cheese
1 pound deer tenderloin	2 tablespoons Tony's seasoning
1/2 cup mushrooms	6 bacon strips

Cut the peppers down one side all the way through and remove the seeds. Chop the deer meat and mushrooms and grate the cheese. Blend the meat, cheese, mushrooms and Tony's seasoning together and stuff the mixture in the peppers. Wrap bacon around the pepper. Then run a toothpick through the bacon to hold it in place while cooking. Cook at 300° F for 3 to 4 hours or smoke for 5 to 6 hours. Then enjoy your deer poppers.

Family Fun - Venison Poppers

My sons, 10 & 11, actually help and do the prep and cooking, they love to cook —Steve Cvetnic, OH

Venison loin or steak
1 package bacon
Honey

Brown sugar
Salt and pepper

Heat oven to 350° F or outside grill to low.

Salt and pepper venison and cut pieces into 2-inch square chunks.

Cut bacon strips in half. Wrap bacon strips around venison.

Place wrapped pieces on non-stick pan or aluminum foil (we use this as an easy throw away for clean up). Leave about 1/2-inch spaces between pieces. If grilling, use foil for sure.

Just pour a few drops of honey on each piece and sprinkle about 1/2 teaspoon of brown sugar on each piece. My son says the more, the better.

Put in oven or on grill for about 1/2 hour or until bacon turns crispy. The crisper the bacon gets, the better it tastes.

Eat 'em warm so the brown sugar melts in mouth....

V-D Poppers

Jay Neumann, TX

1 pound venison pan sausage
15 to 20 jalapeños -
     depending on size
1 package of cream cheese

1 package of bacon
Salt
Pepper
Toothpicks

Brown meat and let cool down a little, add cheese and mix well. I wash my hands real well and then you can mix up the sausage and cream cheese together really well.

Soak toothpicks in water.

Slice peppers and remove seeds and white vein if desired to reduce heat from peppers. Stuff peppers with mix and wrap with bacon. You can use any type of bacon and as much as you like. Use toothpick to stick through bacon to keep it from unwrapping.

If you have any meat/cheese mix leftover, you can put it in bell peppers or poblano peppers and bake or grill.

You can grill them on pit or bake in oven. On grill, cook until bacon is crisp or to your delight. When using oven, bake at 300° F for 20 to 30 minutes. Enjoy with beer or wine.

Backstrap Cannon Balls

Eli Berry, TX

Strips of backstrap
Dry packages of Hidden Valley Ranch Dressing mix
Jalapeños
Bacon
Toothpicks or skewers
Jalapeño jack cheese slices, optional

Powder backstrap strips with dressing powder. Roll jalapeños up in backstrap and wrap with bacon. Secure with toothpicks or skewers. Grill until done.

Option: about a minute before they are ready to come off the grill, top with a piece of the cheese and allow to melt before pulling off grill.

Grilled Cream Cheese Deer Bits

Cory Pruitt, AL

Dale's seasoning
Meat tenderizer
Venison

Bacon
Cream cheese
Toothpicks

Soak venison in Dale's seasoning and meat tenderizer for about 2 to 3 hours before cooking.

Cut venison into 4-inch by 2-inch strips.

Roll a tablespoon of cream cheese into center. Wrap with a piece of bacon. To hold it all together, skewer with a toothpick.

Grill until bacon is crispy on all sides.

Spaghetti Stick Poppers

Paul Guidry

1 pound venison backstrap
1 pound package of bacon
2 - 3 jalapeños
4 ounces cream cheese, frozen
A few sticks of uncooked spaghetti (sub toothpicks)
Optional - marinade or seasoning of choice

    Thinly slice the backstrap, about 1/4-inch thick, across the grain. You can marinate or season the backstrap if you like, but it doesn't really need any extra tenderizing or flavoring. Cut the jalapeños into 1/4-inch wide strips, the same length as the width of your backstrap slices. You can use bigger or smaller slices to change for heat preference. Break the frozen cream cheese block up into small chunks. Place a chunk of cream cheese and a piece of jalapeño on a slice of backstrap, and roll up. Wrap this in a slice of bacon, and skewer with a spaghetti stick. Break off the stick, leaving a little sticking out of each side. Repeat for the remaining slices of backstrap. Grill on high heat until the bacon is cooked. The spaghetti sticks will cook with the juices from the meat, so there is no need to remove them like you would with toothpicks.

Chapter 2

Venison Roasts

Coca-Cola Smoked Venison Roast

Chris Gagnon, NY

4 to 6 pounds deer roast, tenderized
1 cup brown sugar
1 small bottle Colgin Liquid Smoke
1 package Lipton's Beefy Onion Soup mix
1 cup Coca-Cola Classic
1/2 cup salt
1 medium onion, sliced into slivers
1/2 garlic bulb (about 6 cloves), cut into slivers
1 teaspoon cayenne pepper
1 teaspoon black pepper

Add 1/2 bottle of Colgin Liquid Smoke to the tenderized roast making sure all the meat absorbs some of the liquid.

In a bowl, mix the brown sugar, Coca-Cola Classic, salt and the remaining liquid smoke. Pour the brine-sugar-liquid smoke mixture on all sides of the roast and rub in firmly. Turn the meat over every few hours and reapply the brine-sugar-liquid smoke mixture on top. Marinate for 12 hours. Gently wash the marinade off the venison using cold running water.

Using a sharp knife, cut slits throughout the roast for stuffing.

Combine the onion, garlic, ground cayenne pepper and half the Lipton Soup Mix and mix well. Stuff the slits of the roast with this mixture until all of the stuffing is used up. Sprinkle a generous amount of garlic and onion powder, ground black pepper and remaining soup mix on all sides of the roast. Tightly wrap the entire roast onto a large sheet of heavy-duty aluminum foil.

Roast in the oven at 275° F for 3 hours, then at 300° for 2 hours.

Italian Deer

Joe Herkert, IL

3 to 4 pounds deer roast
1 tablespoon dry mustard
1 tablespoon salt
1 tablespoon pepper

1 tablespoon garlic powder
1 tablespoon Worcestershire sauce
1 tablespoon dry Italian seasoning

Place a large venison roast in crock-pot, almost covering with water. Mix the seasoning and spread over roast. Cook until tender. Tear meat apart, cook on low another 60 minutes; may add water at any time if it gets dry. Can be warmed up later for a meal, cookout, or whatever. Can add more water as deer seems to soak it up .This is the easiest Italian beef I've ever made, and the best part is that people who don't like deer meat won't even know it isn't beef.

Venison Hindquarter Roast and Kraut

Jeffrey Heelan, PA

1 venison hindquarter
Two 12-ounce cans of beer
5 pounds bagged sauerkraut
Salt and pepper to taste

2 bay leaves
4 cloves of fresh garlic (sliced pieces)
1/4 cup extra virgin olive oil

Slice small incisions in roast and insert garlic pieces throughout. Heat oil in large pan and brown hindquarter on all sides. Place hindquarter in electric roaster pan, add sauerkraut, beer and enough water to bring liquid up about half way in pan. Cook at 250° F for 7 to 8 hours. Then serve with fresh rye or pumpernickel bread; it will melt in your mouth! Better than pork and kraut!

Cadiz Township Venison Roast

Carey Stevenson, MI

1 large onion, thinly sliced
3 to 4 pounds boneless rolled and tied venison shoulder roast or substitute
1 teaspoon freshly ground pepper
1 clove garlic, minced
1/4 to 1/2 pound side pork, sliced (1/4-inch slices)
1 cup dry red wine

Heat oven to 350° F. Place onion in bottom of 3-quart roasting pan with cover. Place roast on top of onion. Sprinkle roast with pepper and garlic. Arrange side pork slices across roast. Pour wine over roast. Cover tightly. Bake for 2 to 2-1/2 hours, or until meat is tender. Remove cover. Bake for 30 minutes longer. Let roast stand for 10 minutes before serving.

Bacon-Wrapped Venison Roast

Jordan Underhill, TN

4 pounds venison roast
1 teaspoon dried rosemary
1 teaspoon salt
1 teaspoon sugar
1/2 teaspoon cinnamon
1/2 teaspoon black pepper

1/4 teaspoon ginger
1/4 teaspoon cloves
6 thick slices bacon
1 cup red wine
2 tablespoons butter
2 tablespoons bread crumbs

Preheat oven to 350° F.

In a small bowl, combine rosemary, salt, sugar, cinnamon, pepper, ginger, and cloves. Rub mixture evenly over venison roast, patting down to adhere. Wrap bacon slices evenly over roast.

Place roast in a roasting pan; pour wine over. Roast 2-1/2 hours until meat is very soft and internal temperature reaches 150°. Remove roast from pan; transfer to a serving platter.

Place roasting pan over medium heat on stove top; add remaining ingredients and simmer, scraping to mix juices, until thickened. Pour over roast and serve.

Slow Cooker Sweet and Sour Venison Shoulder Roast

David Zachow, WI

1/2 cup ketchup
1/2 cup packed light brown sugar
1/2 cup cider vinegar
1 tablespoon mustard powder

1/2 teaspoon cayenne pepper
Salt and pepper to taste
1 large venison shoulder roast

Wash venison roast well and place in bottom of slow cooker.

In a separate bowl, whisk together remaining ingredients, and pour over roast.

Cook on low for 8 to 10 hours, turning roast once halfway through.

Serve with choice of potato and remaining sauce.

Roasted Venison

Brian Gottschall, TN

3 pounds Denver roast of venison, cut into 6-inch by 3-inch pieces
2 heads garlic, cloves separated and smashed
1/2 cup savory or thyme leaves, lightly crushed
1/2 cup dry red wine
1/4 teaspoon ground allspice
1/2 teaspoon black peppercorns, slightly cracked
1/4 cup plus 1-1/2 tablespoons extra-virgin olive oil, divided
1 tablespoon kosher salt

Toss venison with garlic, savory or thyme, wine, allspice, peppercorns, and 1/4 cup oil in a sealable bag. Marinate, chilled, turning bag occasionally, at least 8 hours.

Bring venison to room temperature, about 1 hour.

Preheat oven to 450°F with rack in middle.

Discard marinade and pat meat dry. Sprinkle on all sides with 1 tablespoon kosher salt, then 1/2 teaspoon ground pepper. Heat remaining 1-1/2 tablespoons oil in a 12-inch heavy skillet over medium-high heat until it shimmers, then brown meat on all sides in 2 or 3 batches, 3 to 4 minutes per batch. Transfer to a shallow baking pan.

Roast until venison registers 125°F on an instant-read thermometer (inserted 2-inches horizontally into meat) for rare, 5 to 8 minutes (depending on thickness of meat). Let stand on a cutting board 10 minutes before slicing across the grain.

Corned Venison Roast

Bill Luell, TX

1/2 gallon water
1 cup kosher salt
1/3 cup sugar
1/2 ounce Instacure No. 1 (sodium nitrite)
1 tablespoon cracked black pepper
1 tablespoon toasted coriander seeds
12 bay leaves, crushed

1 tablespoon red pepper flakes
1 tablespoon dried thyme
1 teaspoon caraway seeds
1 cinnamon stick
6 cloves
5 to 6 garlic cloves, chopped
3 to 5 pounds venison roast

Place everything but the roast in a pot and bring it to a boil. Turn off the heat, cover and let cool to room temperature. This will take a few hours.

Trim any silverskin you find off the roast. Leave the fat.

Once the brine is cool, place the meat in a container just about large enough to hold the roast, and completely cover with the brine. You might have extra brine, which you can discard. I use a clean stone to weigh the meat down. Cover and put in the fridge for 5 to 7 days, depending on the roast size. A 2 pound roast might only need 3 days. The longer it soaks, the saltier it will get; but you want the salt and nitrate to work its way to the center of the roast, and that takes time. Err on extra days, not fewer days.

After the week has passed, you have corned venison. To cook and eat, rinse off the meat, then put the roast in a pot just large enough to hold it and cover with fresh water. You don't want too large a pot or the fresh water will leach out too much flavor from the salty meat, it's an osmosis thing.

Cover and simmer (don't boil) the meat for 3 to 5 hours.

Eat hot or cold. It is absolutely fantastic with good mustard and some sauerkraut on a sandwich.

Venison Yum Roast

Bob Petersen, MS

4 to 5 pounds venison butt roast, trimmed of fat and sinew
1 packet dry onion soup mix
1 can cream of mushroom soup
Fresh ground black pepper

Place roast in crock-pot (or can cover with 3 to 4 layers of aluminum foil). Liberally grind fresh ground black pepper over top of roast. Sprinkle half of the dry onion soup mix, shaken in packet first, over top; only use half as entire packet is too salty. Spread entire can, undiluted, cream of mushroom soup mix over top of roast. Cook in crock-pot on low for 8 hours or in oven at 250°F for 8 hours. Once roast is out of oven, allow to rest for minimum of 20 minutes. Meanwhile, pour drippings and excess soup, etc. into bowl and whisk; makes a superb gravy.

Coffee Roast

Johnny Hatridge, AR

10 cups coffee
2 to 3 pounds deer roast
1 large onion, diced
4 cloves garlic, diced
3 tablespoons olive oil
1 bell pepper, diced

5 red potatoes, cut bite-size
5 carrots, cut bite-size
4 stalks celery, cut bite-size
4 turnips, cut bite-size, optional
1 can cream of mushroom soup
Corn starch

In a large cast iron Dutch oven, heat olive oil and brown roast on all sides. Add onion, garlic, and bell pepper. Pour coffee over roast. Cover and cook in 250° to 300° oven until fork tender. Add potatoes, carrots, celery, turnips and soup. Add corn starch to thicken gravy. Make corn bread, serve hot.

Venison Shoulder Roast

Wade Daily, LA

1 venison shoulder
10 to 12 small red potatoes,
    with skin, halved
1 package button mushrooms
1 pound baby carrots
1 head of cabbage, quartered
1 large onion, sliced 1/8-inch thick

1 bell pepper, ribbon sliced
2 celery stalks, ribbon sliced
2 tablespoons minced garlic
2 brown gravy packets
2 onion soup packets
Worcestershire sauce
Black pepper, salt, Cajun seasoning

Stab the venison shoulder all over with a fork. Season with salt, pepper and minced garlic. Soak with Worcestershire and cover in refrigerator. Leave 2 to 3 hours turning every 30 to 45 minutes.

In a large roaster, place the shoulder in the center. Surround it with potatoes, cabbage, carrots and mushrooms. Place onion, bell pepper and celery on top of roast and veggies. Dust to taste with Cajun seasoning. Mix gravy and onion soup packets, pour over roast and veggies.

Cook in preheated oven for 2 to 3 hours at 350° F.

Venison French Dip

Craig DeVliegher, IN

3 pounds venison roast
2 packets onion soup mix
2 large onions

Provolone cheese
Hoagie buns

Using a pressure cooker or slow cooker depending on time. Make the onion soup mix, add onions, and roast. Cook all day 6 to 8 hours on low in a slow cooker, or 1 hour in pressure cooker. Once done, shred the roast and serve on toasted hoagie buns with melted provolone cheese. Pour some of the juice into small cups for dipping. Extremely simple and basic but it's my families all time favorite.

Ah Sweet Reward

Greg Bailey, KY

1-1/2 to 3 pounds deer roast
4 garlic cloves, chopped
1 large onion
1 pound baby carrots
2 pounds new potatoes or
    golden, chopped

2 tablespoons salt
1 teaspoon pepper
2 cups chicken broth
1/2 cup maple syrup
1 tablespoon cooking oil

Sear roast in oil over high heat on all sides.

Place garlic, onion, potatoes in Dutch oven, then roast, then carrots. Pour chicken stock over all. Salt and pepper to taste.

Bake at 350° F for approximately 90 minutes depending on size of roast. Baste roast at least every 30 minutes.

Remove lid at approximately 10 minutes before finished. Remove 1 cup of juice and mix with syrup. Baste roast, return to stove without lid, and cook until roast and fixings are starting to brown.

Savory Deer Roast

Kim Kelemen, MO

Deer roast
Milk
Salt and pepper
2 cans beef broth
Worcestershire sauce

Potatoes
Carrots
Onion
Celery

Soak deer roast in milk overnight in the fridge, put roast in the crock pot the next morning, discard milk. Layer all the vegetables on the bottom of the crock-pot, place roast on top. Cover roast with 2 cans of beef broth, salt and pepper to taste, a few shakes of the Worcestershire sauce, and enough water to cover the roast. Cook on low for 8 hours.

Paula's Cajun Roast

Jay Carper, TX

Large venison cut
Garlic
Cayenne

Onion
Salt and black pepper
Red wine

Cut regularly spaced narrow holes (about the width of a steak knife) and alternately insert a garlic clove or cayenne pepper into each hole. How much cayenne you use depends on how much you can handle and still taste anything. Put it in the crock-pot with some onion, salt, pepper, and red wine. Cook it all day long.

Chapter 3

Ground Venison

Venison Mushroom and Swiss Burgers

Jim Pickens, WV

1 to 2 pounds ground venison depending on how many people you're feeding
1/2 to 1 cup mushrooms (your choice), diced
1/2 onion, optional
1 package Swiss cheese (not processed), sliced
Buns

In a large mixing bowl, mix the mushrooms and onions into the ground meat. You can use the jarred mushroom gravy for moisture and that authentic restaurant taste.

Form into patties to the thickness you prefer then slow cook to make sure they come out right. Place a slice of cheese on each patty and serve on whatever kind on bun you prefer and enjoy.

Skinless Deer Sausage

Amy Birk, MO

3 pounds ground deer
1 pound ground pork
1 teaspoon black pepper
1 teaspoon mustard powder or seed
3/4 teaspoon garlic powder
4 tablespoons Morton tender quick salt

2 tablespoons brown sugar
*1 tablespoon Worcestershire sauce
*1 tablespoon soy sauce
*1 teaspoon liquid smoke
   (*optional)

Mix well and form into rolls. Wrap each roll in foil and refrigerate 24 hours. Fill the bottom of a broiler pan about half way with water. Prick bottom of each roll and place rolls on top of pan. Bake at 350° F for no more than 50 minutes (less for small diameter rolls). Let cool, unwrap from foil and refrigerate. Makes approximately 6 to 8 rolls (half-dollar diameter).

Hoosier Hamburgers

Mark McMichael, IN   *Serves 6 to 8*

1-1/2 to 2 pounds venison burger
1/4 cup oatmeal (unflavored)
2 teaspoons brown sugar
2 teaspoons vegetable oil

1 package dry onion soup mix
1 tablespoon cumin
1/4 cup steak sauce
Mushrooms - optional

Mix all ingredients in a large mixing bowl. Refrigerate for 2 hours, stirring about every 30 minutes. After the 2 hours, make patties out of the mixture. Using a press works best, use wax paper for separation. Bake or fry according to preference and serve with buns and all condiments desired.

Deer Burger Casserole

Jason Houser, IL

1-1/2 pounds ground venison
1 medium onion, chopped
3 cups cooked egg noodles, drained
One 15-ounce can white kernel corn
One 14 1/2-ounce can cream of chicken soup

1 teaspoon salt
Dash of pepper
Bread crumbs

Brown ground venison and onions together, drain. Cook noodles after meat is brown and onions are tender. Combine meat mixture, noodles, corn, soup, salt and pepper. Stir until mixed well. Sprinkle with bread crumbs. Bake at 350° F for 45 minutes.

Sloppy Does

Jason Houser, IL

1 pound ground venison
1/2 cup onion, chopped
One 10 3/4-ounce can condensed tomato soup
1/4 cup water
1 tablespoon prepared mustard
1/2 teaspoon salt
1/4 teaspoon pepper
6 hamburger buns

In skillet cook meat and onion till meat is browned.
Stir in soup, water, mustard, salt and pepper. Simmer, uncovered, for 2 to 3 minutes. Split and toast buns; serve meat mixture on buns.

Venison Meatloaf

Ronald Lefebvre, GA

2 pounds ground venison
Seasoned bread crumbs
2 eggs
1 small onion, finely chopped
1 can Hunts tomato sauce, Italian style

1 teaspoon Worcestershire sauce
2 carrots, finely chopped
Salt and pepper sparingly
Dash of hot sauce

Mix all ingredients in a bowl by hand, use 1/4 of Hunts tomato sauce to mix with venison, put remaining sauce aside. Fashion into a loaf to fit in a loaf style pan, preheat oven to 350° F, put remaining sauce over loaf and bake for 30 to 35 minutes, serve with mashed potatoes and green beans.

Venison Burgers

Brandi Perez, MI

2 pounds ground venison
1/2 cup diced onion
1/3 cup Worcestershire sauce
1 teaspoon garlic (crushed or powder)

1 teaspoon black pepper
1 package saltine crackers, crushed
1 egg

Combine all ingredients and make patties. Grill to your liking. Serve on a warm, toasted bun.

Steak Fingers

Tommy Meinen, TX

1 pound ground deer meat
3 eggs, scrambled
Salt and pepper

Tony Chacheres Creole Seasoning
Flour

Make small steak fingers out of meat. Dip into eggs, roll in flour and deep fry. Add salt, pepper, and Tony Chacheres to taste. Serve with mashed potatoes, white peppered gravy and green beans. Top meat with gravy.

Note: I use ground meat instead of backstrap because of gristle and tenderness.

Deer Burgers in Gravy (Crock-Pot)

Matthew Saxsma, AR

1 pound ground deer meat
1/2 cup seasoned bread crumbs
Salt and pepper
1 large can or 2 small cans
  cream of mushroom soup

Oil for cooking meat
1/2 cup milk
1 onion, sliced
1 egg

Mix meat, bread crumbs, egg, salt and pepper.

Patty meat mixture into slider-size burgers. Fry quickly in pan with a little oil (a quick brown on each side, don't over cook). Cook onion in same pan. Add onion and burgers to crock-pot. Mix milk and mushroom soup, pour over onion and burgers. Let cook a few hours, until very tender (this is a very simple recipe, but it's the best; it goes with everything and it tastes great.)

Venison Bean Hash

Steven Woldt, WI

2 pounds ground venison
1 large onion, diced
One 28-ounce can pork & beans

2 cups ketchup
Salt and pepper to taste

Brown the venison and drain. Add onion, pork and beans, and ketchup. Simmer 30 to 45 minutes. Season to taste. Serve on buttered bread or eat plain.

High-Speed Beef Burgers

Requires the use of a small home counter top meat grinder but it's worth it.
— Tom "Painful" McDermott, TN

Venison
Bulk Italian sausage
Onions

Garlic
Seasonings
Onion Kaiser rolls

The mixture of venison to Italian sausage is around 2 to 1. That's 2 pounds venison to 1 pound Italian sausage. If you like it a bit dryer, add less Italian sausage. Run the meats through a grinder with or without onions and garlic...works both ways. Form into patties, season and barbecue them to your liking.

In a small frying pan, brown onions and garlic. Place cooked patties on a roll and top with the browned onions and garlic. If you want mustard or any other stuff on them, go for it. Now, crack an ice cold Miller beer and your ready to eat.

Shipwreck Casserole

Jason Houser, IL

1 pound ground venison
1 pound onions, sliced
3 potatoes, sliced

Salt and pepper, to taste
One 15-ounce can kidney beans, drained
One 10 3/4-ounce can tomato soup

In a 9-inch by 9-inch baking dish or crock-pot, layer half the meat, onion and potatoes. Salt and pepper to taste. Layer same 3 ingredients again. Top with beans and soup. Bake 1 hour at 350° F, or cook 5 to 6 hours in crock-pot on slow heat.

Venison Meatballs

Bobby Holmes, VA

1 pound ground deer meat
2 slices fresh white bread,
    ground into crumbs
1 egg
1/2 teaspoon onion powder
1 teaspoon garlic powder

2 teaspoons oregano
1 teaspoon basil
1 teaspoon salt
1/4 teaspoon ground pepper
1/8 cup Parmesan cheese
1/3 cup milk

Soak the fresh bread crumbs in the milk. Add all the remaining ingredients, mix by hand until all ingredients are blended, but do not over mix. Form into balls. Two methods for cooking: 1) brown them in a pan with a little oil, then finish them in your favorite marinara sauce. 2) Preheat oven to 450° F and bake them until cooked through. Time depends on how big you make your meatballs.

Venison Manicotti

Andrew Roney, WA

4 teaspoons olive oil
1 medium onion, coarsely chopped
1 pound ground venison
Salt and freshly ground black pepper
One 8-ounce package manicotti
One 15-ounce container whole-milk ricotta
3 cups shredded mozzarella
1 cup grated Parmesan
2 tablespoons chopped fresh Italian parsley leaves
2 garlic cloves, minced
3 cups marinara sauce
2 tablespoons butter, cut into pieces

Heat a heavy-medium skillet over medium heat. Add 1 teaspoon of the olive oil, onion and ground venison. Season with salt and pepper. Saute until the meat browns and the onion is translucent, about 5 minutes. Remove from heat and cool.

Brush 1 teaspoon of oil over a large baking sheet. Cook the manicotti in a large pot of boiling salted water until slightly softened, but still very firm to the bite, about 4 to 6 minutes. Using a slotted spoon, transfer the manicotti from the pot to the oiled baking sheet and cool.

Meanwhile, combine the ricotta, 1 1/2 to 2 cups mozzarella cheese, 1/2 cup Parmesan, and parsley. Add the garlic, salt, and pepper to taste, and mix.

Stir the cooled meat mixture into the cheese mixture.

Preheat the oven to 350° F.

Brush the remaining 2 teaspoons of oil over a 13 by 9 by 2-inch glass baking dish. Spoon 1 1/2 cups of the marinara sauce over the bottom of the prepared dish. Fill the manicotti with the cheese-meat mixture. Arrange the stuffed pasta in a single layer in the prepared dish and spoon the remaining sauce over.

Sprinkle the remaining 1 1/2 ups of mozzarella cheese, then the remaining 1/2 cup of Parmesan over the stuffed pasta. Dot entire dish with the butter pieces. Bake the manicotti uncovered until heated through and the sauce bubbles on the sides of the dish, about 30 to 35 minutes. Let the manicotti stand 5 minutes and serve.

Venison Spanish Rice

Chris Lippincott, NY

1 pound ground venison or venison sausage
1 cup of dry white rice
1 can of diced tomatoes
1 jar of medium salsa
1 small onion, diced
3 cloves of garlic, diced
1 small green pepper, diced
1 can of black olives, slice as many as you'd like for taste
1 teaspoon of cilantro
8-ounces of shredded Mexican cheese

Cook rice to directions. Saute the venison, garlic, onion, and peppers. Drain the meat mixture. In a large casserole dish, mix the rice, meat mixture, tomatoes, salsa, olives and cilantro. Cook in a 350° F oven for 30 minutes. Top with cheese and continue to cook another 15 minutes. Serve with a salad or green vegetable.

Mom's Montana Venison Spaghetti

D Rogers, CA

Venison burger
Onion
Rotel
Can of traditional spaghetti sauce

Salt
Pepper
Anaheim chili
Pasta of choice

Cook up the burger with onions and salt and pepper. Cook up the pasta al dente or not too soft (nobody likes limp noodles). Take all other ingredients and blend them. Pour the sauce into the drained meat
Serve with noodles and cheese of choice.

Venison Breakfast Sausage

Clay Whittaker, IN

1 pound ground venison
1/2 pound pepper bacon, cut into small pieces
1 teaspoon monosodium glutamate (such as Ac'cent)
1 tablespoon garlic powder
1 tablespoon onion powder
1 teaspoon ground mustard
1 tablespoon ground chipotle
1 teaspoon salt
1 teaspoon anise seed
1 teaspoon fennel seed
1 teaspoon crushed red pepper flakes
1 teaspoon dried parsley

In a large bowl, thoroughly combine the venison, bacon, monosodium glutamate, garlic, onion, mustard, chipotle, salt, anise, fennel, red pepper flakes, and parsley. Grind the mixture through a small plate in a meat grinder. Refrigerate until ready to use.

Taco Pie

Jim Lanhardt, IL

2 pounds ground deer
2 packages taco seasoning
1 tube crescent rolls
1-1/2 cups crushed Doritos (taco flavor)

1 cup water
1 cup sour cream
1 cup shredded cheddar

Brown deer meat, drain. Stir in seasoning and water, simmer 5 minutes. Spread rolls to cover bottom of 10-inch pan. Sprinkle 1 cup Doritos over rolls. Place meat mixture over top of chips. Spread sour cream over meat. Cover with cheese. Top with remaining Doritos. Cook at 375° F for 25 minutes.

Mushroom and Cheese-Stuffed Venison Loaf

Clay Whittaker, IN

2 pounds ground venison
1 onion, chopped
One 6-ounce box dry instant stuffing mix
2 eggs, beaten
2 tablespoons Worcestershire sauce
2 tablespoons ketchup
1/4 cup spicy tomato-vegetable juice cocktail (such as V8) (optional)
1 teaspoon prepared yellow mustard
10 ounces fresh morel mushrooms
8 slices sharp Cheddar cheese
6 slices bacon
1/2 cup barbecue sauce (such as Sweet Baby Ray's®)
2 tablespoons grated Parmesan cheese (optional)
1 pinch salt and ground black pepper, or to taste

Preheat oven to 350° F (175° C).

Mix ground venison, onion, stuffing mix, eggs, Worcestershire sauce, ketchup, vegetable juice cocktail, and yellow mustard in a large bowl with your hands until thoroughly combined.

Place half the venison mixture into a 9 by 11-inch casserole dish; pat the meat mixture into an even layer.

Spread morel mushrooms over meat; top with cheddar cheese slices.

Spread remaining half of venison mixture over cheese slices; pat down to form an even layer and press the edges together to seal in the mushrooms and cheese.

Arrange bacon slices over the meatloaf; spread barbecue sauce evenly over the loaf. Sprinkle with Parmesan cheese.

Bake in the preheated oven until the meatloaf is browned and an instant-read meat thermometer inserted into the thickest part of the loaf reads 160° F (70° C), about 1 hour and 15 minutes.

Drain excess grease and allow loaf to stand for 5 minutes before serving.

Chapter 4

Venison Steaks

Zesty Backstraps

Clay Justice, MS

1/2 backstrap
1 cup zesty Italian salad dressing
1 cup self rising flour

1/4 cup corn meal
Vegetable oil

Cut backstrap in 1/2-inch steaks. Place meat in a bowl with water covering. Refrigerator changing water 3 times a day for 2 days, meat will not be red or have a game taste.

Pour water out and replace with zesty Italian dressing. Let marinate overnight and the next day or 2.

Remove directly out of dressing and cover with the flour/corn meal mixed. Heat vegetable oil in skillet 1/4-inch deep on high.

Put steaks in and flip after 45 seconds. Turn heat down to not burn oil, medium heat for 2 more minutes each side.

Serve with coleslaw and garden tomatoes.

Grilled Venison Backstrap

Tim Hylton, MI

Venison chunks
Apple cider
Barbecue sauce

Bacon
Toothpicks
Olive oil

Place chunks of venison into a shallow baking dish, and pour enough apple cider in to cover them. Cover and refrigerate for 2 hours. Remove and pat dry. Discard apple cider and return venison to the dish. Pour barbecue sauce over the chunks, cover and refrigerate for 2 to 3 more hours.

Preheat an outdoor grill for high heat. Charcoal is best, but if you must, use gas. Remove meat from the refrigerator, and let stand for 30 minutes or until no longer chilled. Wrap each chunk of venison in a slice of bacon, and secure with toothpicks.

Brush the grill grate with olive oil when hot, and place venison pieces on the grill so they are not touching. The bacon will kick up some flames, so be ready. Grill, turning occasionally, until the bacon becomes slightly burnt, 15 to 20 minutes.

Steak Yum

Eugene Przybyl, NY

1 thick cut steak
1/2 cup vinegar

2 cups soy sauce
5 garlic cloves

Take a thick cut steak and make cuts in the meat big enough to stuff garlic clove into. Then mix 1/2 cup vinegar with 2 cups soy sauce and let steak marinade over night. Grill or pan fry them the next day.

Mesquite Grilled Sweet & Spicy Venison Steak

Sam Muro, OR

Venison steaks of your choice
Salt and pepper
Garlic powder
Cumin powder
Mexican oregano

1 jar of Tabasco jalapeño jelly
1/2 cup of tequila
2 tablespoons of lime juice
Mesquite wood chips (for BBQ)

Season the venison steaks with the salt, pepper, garlic powder, cumin powder and Mexican oregano.

In a sauce pan, add the jalapeño jelly. Add the tequila and lime juice. Over medium heat, whisk till smooth. It will make a glaze, then remove from heat.

Place the venison steaks on the grill. Cook one side; flip and brush with glaze; then repeat on the other side.

You can serve with a green salad and grilled corn on the cob. Brush the glaze on the corn for a tasty treat. Enjoy this tasty southwest style meal.

Easiest & Best Country-Fried Steak

Gregg Nowell, TN

Venison backstrap
Zick's venison seasoning

Flour
Peanut oil

Slice backstrap in 1/2-inch thick pieces, across the grain. Cube or tenderize venison steaks. Sprinkle liberally on both sides with Zick's venison seasoning. Coat with flour. Heat no more than 1/2-inch deep peanut oil to 350° F in a large skillet; cast iron is best. Fry steaks 20 to 30 seconds on each side, turning twice. Pour off all but 4 tablespoons of the oil, turn down heat, add 2 to 3 heaping tablespoons of flour and stir until brown, being careful not to burn. Add 1 cup of cold water and stir until gravy is the consistency you want. Serve with mashed potatoes or rice. The two "secrets" to this is using peanut oil and frying hot and fast.

Ultimate Grilled Backstrap Steaks

Rick Ford, OK

Venison backstraps, cut into 6-ounce steaks
Worcestershire sauce
Louisiana hot sauce
McCormick Grillmates Montreal Steak seasoning
Salt and pepper

Marinate venison steaks overnight in a mixture of 1 part Worcestershire to 2 parts Louisiana Hot Sauce (enough to completely cover all steaks). Remove and lightly salt and pepper venison steaks. Thoroughly dust with McCormick Grillmates Montreal Steak seasoning, and grill over an open charcoal or wood flame. This is also very good as a kabob meat with red and green bell peppers, onions, and fresh jalapeños.

Momma's Deer Steaks

Christina Mazurkiewicz, MO

Venison steak
Jack Daniel's
Steak seasoning
Chop sprinkle onion
Strips of pepper bacon

Marinate steaks with Jack Daniel's, just enough to cover it for 1 hour. Add steak seasoning to bring out the taste. Add chop sprinkle onion. Wrap pepper bacon around steaks and secure it with tooth picks. Cover steaks. Slow cook for 1 1/2 hours until well done. Cook in oven 350° F to 375°.

Sunday Venison Steak

David Conn, OH

1 cup flour
2 tablespoons garlic powder
2 tablespoons salt or to your taste
1 tablespoon pepper or to your taste

Two 4-ounce cans mushrooms or fresh mushrooms
2 cans beef broth
2 packets brown gravy mix
2 tablespoons onion powder or 1 large onion, chopped
Four to six 6-ounce venison steaks

In a gallon zip-lock bag, mix flour, garlic powder, salt, pepper, onion powder. Put the steak into the bag and shake until it is well covered.

Heat a large frying pan with cooking oil that covers the bottom, brown both sides of steak. If you choose to use fresh mushrooms and onion, saute them also.

Transport the steak into crock-pot, add the mushrooms and onions, dry gravy mix and beef broth. Cook on high for about 2 to 3 hours until the steak is tender. Serve with your favorite potatoes or rice, salad, and vegetable. Serves 4 to 6 people.

Venison Steaks or Chops

Tom Miller, PA

Flour
Butter
Chicken stock

Onion, chopped
Green pepper, chopped

Dredge meat in flour. Brown meat in butter in cast iron skillet. Add a can of chicken stock. Simmer for 1 hour. Add some onion and green peppers. Cook until vegetables are tender.

Venison Swiss Steaks

Terry Belisle, VA

6 venison steaks, tenderized, about 1/2 pound each
1/2 cup flour
1/2 teaspoon salt and pepper (divided)
3 tablespoons cooking oil
2 large onions, cut into 1/4-inch thick slices
4 cups of stewed tomatoes
1 teaspoon paprika

Preheat the oven to 325° F. Combine the flour, salt, pepper and paprika. Dredge the venison steaks in the seasoned flour mixture, coating both sides. Heat a heavy frying pan over medium-high heat, add the oil, and brown both sides of the steaks. Don't crowd the steaks when browning...it's best to brown 1 or 2 at a time.

Place the browned venison steaks in a large, lidded baking dish and add the remaining ingredients mixing a bit to get some of the tomato and onion under the steaks. Cover and bake for 2 to 3 hours, or until the meat is falling apart tender.

Before serving, give the pot of venison swiss steak a final stir to break up the meat a little. Serve over garlic mashed potatoes or hot buttered noodles.

Bacon Wrapped Venison Loins and Spinach Cakes

Andrew Roney, WA

Spinach and Cheese Cakes:
2 packages frozen chopped spinach, 10 ounces each
3 tablespoons extra-virgin olive oil, 1 for onion, 2 tablespoons to fry cakes
1 small onion, chopped
1/2 cup Italian bread crumbs, 3 handfuls
1/3 cup grated Parmigiano-Reggiano, 2 handfuls
1 egg, beaten
1/4 teaspoon freshly grated nutmeg, coarse salt and freshly ground pepper

4 thin slices bacon
4 venison tenderloin steaks, 1-1/2-inch thick
Coarse salt and cracked black pepper, season to your taste
2 tablespoons butter, divided
1 tablespoon all-purpose flour
1/2 cup dry red wine
1/2 cup beef stock

Plate Garnish:
4 small Roma tomatoes
Extra-virgin oil, for drizzling
2 tablespoons chopped or snipped fresh chives

Defrost spinach in microwave. Wring spinach dry by nesting in kitchen towel and twisting towel over sink until spinach has given off all of it's liquid. Place spinach in a medium mixing bowl. Heat a nonstick skillet over medium heat, add oil and onion and saute the onion until soft, 5 minutes.

Add onion to spinach in bowl and return pan to stove top. Turn off heat. Add remaining ingredients to spinach: bread crumbs, cheese, egg, nutmeg, salt and pepper. Combine mixture with a fork, then form into 3-inch patties. Set aside.

Line bacon up on meat-safe cutting board a few inches apart. Preheat a second skillet over high heat. Reheat the spinach cakes skillet over medium-high heat.

Season steaks with salt and pepper and set on bacon slices in the center of each slice. Wrap bacon over steaks. Place seam side down in pan and cook 2 minutes on each side.

Add 2 tablespoons oil to spinach cakes pan and set cakes in to cook. Work in 2 batches if necessary. Cook cakes 3 minutes on each side.

Reduce heat to medium under steaks after the first 2 minutes on each side. Cook meat another 6 to 10 minutes, turning occasionally, for medium-rare to medium-well.

Remove meat from the pan and let it rest. Add 1 tablespoon of the butter and flour and cook together 1 minute. Whisk in wine and deglaze pan. Whisk in broth and thicken sauce, 1 minute. Add remaining tablespoon of butter and remove skillet from heat.

Quarter tomatoes lengthwise.

To serve, set the spinach cakes and steaks beside each other on 2/3 of serving plates and pour sauce evenly over steaks. Scatter a quartered tomato next to spinach cakes on each plate. Drizzle tomatoes with oil, season with salt and pepper and top with chopped chives. Serve plates immediately.

Bacon-Wrapped Deer Steaks

David Moore, TN

Deer steak (your choice, 1-inch or thicker - I like backstrap)
Bacon
Apple juice
Cornstarch
Sea salt

Toothpicks
Cast iron skillet
Oven capable of 450° F or hotter

Marinate steak in apple juice for 2 hours.

Remove from marinade and wrap with bacon; pin in place with toothpick. Pat dry with paper towels, coat top and bottom with a mixture of corn starch and sea salt. Place on wire rack in freezer for 30 minutes.

Pre-heat cast iron skillet in oven at 450° F to 500°. Remove skillet from oven and place on stove top on highest setting.

Sear steaks in skillet on stove for 2 minutes per side, then place back in oven at 350° until bacon is cooked as desired (Can alternately be finished off on the top rack of your grill if you want to add a smoked flavor.) Let steaks rest, then serve.

Tender Venison

Bob Abel, IA

2 pounds venison steak
1 large onion, chopped
1 teaspoon garlic powder
1 teaspoon ground pepper

1/2 teaspoon salt
1 cup all-purpose flour
1 can cream of mushroom soup
1 can cream of celery soup

Cut venison steak into 2 by 2-inch pieces and tenderize. Mix all ingredients, except flour and venison, in a bowl. Coat venison with flour and brown in a skillet. Layer fried venison and soup mixture in a crock-pot. Cook on high for 1 hour, then cook on low for 4 hours. Serve over boiled potatoes. Garnish with chopped parsley.

Venison Steak with Morel Mushrooms

Mike Marsh, MI   *Serves 4*

2 pounds venison steak
1 tablespoon oil
1/4 cup cognac
1/2 pound fresh morels or 1 ounce dried

1 cup heavy cream
1/3 cup veal or chicken stock
Salt and pepper

If using dried morels soak in cold water for 15 to 20 minutes. Rinse mushrooms and add to skillet with cream. Bring to a boil then reduce heat to simmer until the cream is reduced by half. Pan-fry the steak in olive oil for 4 to 5 minutes on one side and about 3 on the other (don't overcook!). Remove the steak to a plate and deglaze the pan with cognac and stock then add cream and morels and let simmer for a few minutes. Season with salt and pepper. Serve over sliced meat.

Big Game Pie

George Eliopoulos, WI

Potatoes	Greek seasoning
Celery	Garlic powder
Onion	Cheese, shredded
1 pound venison steak	

Brown 1 pound venison steak; cut up into 1/2-inch pieces. Boil potatoes and mash, or use instant mashed potatoes. Then, cut up celery and onion. Lay steak in the bottom of a glass baking dish and sprinkle in onion, celery, greek seasoning and garlic powder to taste. Spread potatoes over the above listed ingredients, until you cannot see them. Sprinkle shredded cheese on top and bake for 45 minutes at 350° F covered with aluminum foil.

Easy Venison Steak Sandwiches

Phil Woiak, WI

2 to 3 pounds boneless venison steak (or chops) sliced no more than 1/4-inch thick
    (you should tenderize the steaks if there from an older animal or are tougher cut)
1 stick margarine - NOT butter (butter burns too easy)
1 large or 2 medium onions, sliced 1/4-inch thick
Crushed garlic
Salt and pepper
12-inch cast iron skillet (must be cast iron!)
Your choice of bread or rolls

Heat the cast iron skillet on medium high BEFORE you add the stick of margarine, then add it! Let the margarine heat until well melted. Then start layering, begin with the chops or steaks, then salt and pepper, then layer onions. On the onions layer more steak, salt and pepper. Repeat the steak, salt, pepper and onions, till they are all in the skillet. When it starts to simmer start turning the whole mix. Then add a teaspoon of crushed garlic. Stir often (every couple of minutes). When the onions are well cooked and the gravy has formed, it is done! There should not be a lot of gravy, let it thicken on it's own as it cooks. Serve on the bread of your choice! Rolls, toast, or plain white bread, whatever you like! This is the recipe that everyone loves even those that say they don't eat venison. This has fed a lot of big eaters, and I mean big boys; college basketball player's, several well over 6-feet tall and boys up to 350 pounds, as well as the ladies, they love it too! This is great for cold days after ice fishing, or long cold sits on a late season deer stand!

Faith's Game-Gone-Wild Venison Backstraps

Faith Perakis, IL

1 venison backstrap
2 bottles of beer
1 package grocery store steak marinade/seasoning (McCormick)
Garlic powder
Onion powder
Bacon

Put backstrap in plastic container filled with both bottles of beer. Soak over night or for 1 day in refrigerator covered. Beer is a natural tenderizer and does help take the gamey taste out. When ready to prepare, pull venison backstraps out of plastic and place on cutting board. Rub backstraps with olive oil. Sprinkle onion and garlic powder over both sides liberally. Then open the package of McCormick steak seasoning/ marinade. RUB the seasoning all over backstrap. Cutting in thick fillets, wrap bacon around each one and secure with toothpick. Cover and return to refrigerator until charcoal is ready. Make sure the coals are low heat.... you do not want to grill them too quickly; this will result in burnt outside and raw inside. So.... Cook at between 250° F to 300°.

Make sure you DO NOT leave the grill! You do not want to over cook venison as it does become tough. Cook on each side 3 to 4 minutes at a time and check to see if you need longer, depending upon the burgundy color inside. Serve with a nice baked potato and salad, you've got a fabulous meal!

Jacked-Up Venison

Benjamin Black, PA

2 pounds venison steaks	1/4 cup chopped/sliced green onions
1/4 cup Jack Daniel's	1/4 cup soy sauce
1/8 cup dijon mustard	1/2 teaspoon of black pepper
1 teaspoon sesame oil	3 to 5 cloves of garlic
1/2 teaspoon Worcestershire sauce	1 onion
1/4 cup dark brown sugar	1/4 teaspoon of cayenne pepper

Finely chop the onion and press the garlic.

Mix the Jack Daniel's, mustard, sesame oil, Worcestershire sauce, brown sugar, green onions, soy sauce, onion, garlic, black pepper and cayenne pepper in a bowl.

Be careful with the cayenne pepper. I prefer a little kick so I usually add more than a quarter teaspoon, but that is a good place to start until you are familiar with how it affects the marinade.

Place the steaks into a 1 gallon plastic bag and carefully dump the contents of the bowl into the bag on top of the steak. Make sure that the steaks are thoroughly covered with the marinade. Let the marinade sit in the fridge for no less than 2 hours.

Fire up the grill and throw the steaks on. Make sure that both sides receive equal attention from the flames. Check regularly to ensure that the meat is done, but not over-cooked.

Red Wine Marinated Flank Steak

Andrew Roney, WA

4 shallots, coarsely chopped	1/4 pound thinly sliced prosciutto
1 cup dry red wine (Cabernet)	1/4 pound thinly sliced Fontina cheese
1/4 cup olive oil	14 fresh basil leaves
2 pounds flank steak, butterflied	Olive oil
Salt and pepper	Cabernet-Shallot Reduction

Whisk together shallots, wine and olive oil in a large baking dish. Add the steak and turn to coat. Cover and refrigerate for at least 4 hours or overnight.

Heat grill to high. Remove the steak from the marinade and blot with paper towels. Lay on a flat surface, cut side up, and season with salt and pepper. Cover the surface with the prosciutto slices, then top with the cheese and a layer of basil leaves. Starting with the side facing you, tightly roll up the steak around the filling. Using kitchen string, tie the roll in 4 or 5 places. Brush the outside of the steak with oil and season with salt and pepper.

Grill the steak over high heat until browned all over, 8 to 10 minutes. Turn the steak 4 times as it cooks. Move the meat away from the direct heat and grill for 15 to 20 minutes, or until an instant-read thermometer registers 125°F for medium-rare. Remove from the grill and let rest 5 minutes before slicing. Slice against the grain into 1/2-inch thick slices and drizzle with the Cabernet-Shallot Reduction.

Cabernet-Shallot Reduction:

2 teaspoons olive oil	1 teaspoon black peppercorns
3 shallots, finely chopped	Salt
1 bottle Cabernet wine	1 tablespoon honey

Heat oil in a large saucepan on the grates of the grill over high heat. Add the shallots and cook until soft. Add the wine and peppercorns, bring to a boil and cook until thickened and reduced to 1 cup. Strain the mixture into a bowl and season with salt, to taste, and honey.

Chapter 5

Venison Kabobs & Skewers

Pineapple-Teriyaki Kabobs

David E. Tusch, MS

1 can pineapple juice
10 ounces Teriyaki sauce
1 backstrap cut in chunks for kabobs
1 onion
1 bell peppers
Cherry tomatoes
Kabob sticks

Mix the 10-ounce bottle of teriyaki sauce with one can of pineapple juice in a bowl. Add venison backstraps and marinate overnight or longer. Cut up your vegetables. When the meat is done marinating, make up the kabob sticks. Cook on a charcoal grill.

Roll Ups

John Vinson, MS

1 backstrap cut to slice
Bacon
Cream cheese
Jalapeño's

Dale's steak seasoning sauce
Rendezvous seasoning
Shish kabob sticks

Marinate the backstrap slices in Dale's steak seasoning sauce with garlic and onion powder for 24 hours. Then take the meat slices, spread on cream cheese, add jalapeño to the middle, and roll it up like a sleeping bag. Wrap a piece of bacon around it and continue until the kabobs are full (probably 4 or 5 on each). Cook to the side of the direct flame until the venison reaches your liking. It usually only takes about 5 to 10 minutes on each side to be just right! Pull off the grill, add rendezvous seasoning and do the fun part: Eat!

Deer Kabobs

George Brumfield, MS

Deer meat, cut into chunks
Mushrooms
Onions
Pineapple, cut into chunks
Cherry tomatoes

Sweet potatoes
Italian dressing (fat free)
Onion powder
Brown sugar

In fat free Italian dressing and onion powder, soak the deer meat chunks for 24 hours. Cut onions and sweet potatoes into chunks. Season the sweet potatoes with brown sugar. Place pineapples, tomatoes, onions, sweet potatoes, and deer meat on metal skewers. Cook on grill for 5 to 10 minutes or until done.

Deer Kabobs

Mark Buchanan, IL

Deer sliced 1/8-inch to 1/4-inch thick
Italian dressing   Bacon

Slice deer, pour Italian dressing over. Place in refrigerator, the longer the better. I do mine 12-24 hours before cooking. Stir every 4-6 hours. On cooking day, take out each strip, rolled. Wrap with 1/3 strip bacon and place on skewer leaving small space between slice. Cook on grill 15-20 minutes. Great with veggie kabobs.

Shrimp and Venison Skewers

Andrew Roney, WA

2 sticks unsalted butter, at room temperature
5 scallions, pale green and white parts only, finely chopped
3 cloves garlic, minced
3 tablespoons soy sauce
Skewers:
1/3 cup extra-virgin olive oil
4 cloves garlic, minced
1 teaspoon kosher salt
1 teaspoon freshly ground black pepper
8 ounces (about 12) medium-size button or cremini mushrooms, halved
1 pound (about 28) large shrimp, peeled and deveined
1 pound venison steak, about 3/4-inch thick, cut into 28 (1-inch) pieces
20 wooden skewers, soaked in water for 30 minutes to prevent scorching

For the butter: In a food processor, combine the butter, scallions, garlic, and soy sauce. Pulse until smooth. Place the mixture on a piece of plastic wrap and form into a log about 1-inch in diameter and 7 inches long. Roll the log in the plastic wrap and refrigerate until firm enough to slice, about 30 minutes. Slice into 1/4-inch pieces.

For the skewers: In a small bowl, mix together the olive oil, garlic, salt, and pepper. Thread 4 pieces of mushroom onto 6 of the skewers. Thread 4 shrimp onto 7 of the skewers. Thread 4 pieces of the meat onto the remaining 7 skewers. Arrange the skewers in a single layer on 2 baking sheets. Spoon the oil mixture over the top and marinate for 15 minutes.

Place a grill pan over medium-high heat or preheat a gas or charcoal grill. Grill the venison skewers for 2 minutes each side for medium. Let the meat rest for 5 minutes. Grill the shrimp skewers for 2 minutes each side until opaque and cooked through. Grill the mushroom skewers for 4 minutes each side until tender. Arrange the skewers on a platter and serve with the sliced butter.

Venison Steakabobs

Pastor Ted Ricci, OH

2 pounds cubed venison
2 teaspoons Montreal Steak Seasoning
1 tablespoon garlic powder (not garlic salt)
1/2 cup olive oil
1/2 cup soy sauce
2 green, red or yellow peppers

16 to 20 whole fresh mushrooms
1 small zucchini
1 large onion
1 pint cherry tomatoes
3 tablespoons lemon juice
Salt and pepper

Sprinkle cubed venison with Montreal Steak seasoning & garlic powder. Put aside for 20 minutes. Mix the olive oil, soy sauce and lemon juice. Pour over the meat. Cover and let it sit in the refrigerator for 1 hour, turning the meat every 15 minutes. Add the vegetables in the last 15 minutes. Turn on your grill. Thread the meat and vegetables onto the skewers, mixing up the pieces. Turn often as you grill and brush on the remaining sauce. Cook for about 12 minutes or until your steakabobs are to your liking. Add salt and pepper to taste and enjoy yourself.

Venison and Shrimp Kabob

David Ames, WI

1 venison loin steak, cut in small pieces
1/2 pound uncooked shrimp
Spicy Italian dressing

Crushed pineapple
Melted butter

Combine all ingredients in zip bag, and marinate for 4 hours, or overnight — the longer the better. Alternate the venison and shrimp on wet kabob sticks and cook in a smoker or charcoal grill.

Grilled Bacon-Wrapped Venison Skewers

Matthew Smith, PA

Venison choice cuts
Fish or shrimp
Bacon

Your favorite seasoning or marinade
Your favorite vegetables

Just cut the deer meat into manageable chunks, then wrap a strip of bacon around it and stick it onto a skewer. Sometimes I like to alternate it with other meat like some sort of fish, shrimp, or the occasional vegetable. You can season the meat with your favorite seasonings or marinades. The only other step is to put the skewers on the grill. Depending on your grilling style, time will vary, but I cook them until the bacon is cooked. The meat will be tender and full of bacon juice.

Venison Kabobs

Andrew Roney, WA

1-1/2 to 2 pounds venison
3 cloves garlic, minced
2 teaspoons smoked paprika
1/2 teaspoon ground turmeric
1 teaspoon ground cumin

1 teaspoon kosher salt
1/2 teaspoon freshly ground black pepper
1/3 cup red wine vinegar
1/2 cup olive oil
4 (12-inch) metal skewers

Cut the beef into 1-1/2 to 1-3/4-inch cubes and place into a large mixing bowl. Set aside.

In the bowl of a food processor combine the garlic, paprika, turmeric, cumin, salt, pepper and red wine vinegar. With the processor running drizzle in the olive oil.

Pour the marinade over the meat and toss to coat. Place in the refrigerator in an airtight container or a sealable plastic bag and allow to marinate for 2 to 4 hours.

Preheat the grill to medium-high heat. Thread the meat onto the skewers leaving about 1/2-inch in between the pieces of meat. Place on the grill and cook, with lid lowered, 2 to 3 minutes per side, 8 to 12 minutes in all (8 minutes for rare and 12 for medium). Remove from the heat to aluminum foil, wrap and allow to rest for 2 to 3 minutes prior to serving.

Garlic-Mustard Grilled Venison Skewers

Andrew Roney, WA

Garlic-Mustard Glaze:
4 cloves garlic, finely chopped
1/4 cup grainy mustard
2 tablespoon dijon mustard
2 teaspoons Spanish paprika
1/4 teaspoon kosher salt

1/4 teaspoon freshly ground black
   pepper
1 tablespoon low-sodium soy sauce
2 tablespoons white wine vinegar
1 tablespoon honey
1 pound venison, cut into slices

Whisk together all ingredients in a small bowl. Cover and let sit at room temperature for 30 minutes before using. Skewer the meat onto skewers so that it lies flat. Brush the meat liberally on both sides with the Garlic-Mustard Glaze. Grill the meat for 2 to 3 minutes per side until golden brown and cooked to medium-rare doneness, brushing with the remaining glaze while grilling. Remove from grill and serve.

Deer Rollups

Casey Rose, MS

1 pound venison backstrap or tenderloin cut into 1-inch cubes
1 pound smoked bacon
Cream cheese
Sliced jalapeños
Dale's steak seasoning

Marinate the cubed venison for approximately 2 hours in the Dales sauce. Take a cube of venison, add a dollop of cream cheese and a slice of jalapeño and wrap it in enough of the bacon to go around it one time just overlapping slightly. Put rollups on skewers on grill at 350° for approximately 45 minutes.

Grilled Venison Kabobs with Pesto Marinade

Doug Thalacker, IN

1 tablespoon basil pesto (recipe below)
1 tablespoon oregano pesto

1/2 teaspoon dried rosemary
1/2 teaspoon crushed chili peppers
1 tablespoon minced onion
2 tablespoons lemon juice
2 tablespoons olive oil or 1 tablespoon each, olive oil and sesame seed oil
1-1/2 to 2 pounds venison, cut into 1-inch pieces.
1 red, green and yellow pepper, cut into 1-inch pieces
1 onion, cut into 1-inch pieces
1 to 2 mushrooms, without stems

Tomato-Basil Pesto
1-1/2 to 2 cups fresh basil leaves
4 to 5 sun-dried tomatoes
2 to 3 garlic cloves
2 tablespoons grated romano cheese
6 tablespoons grated parmesan cheese
1/3 cup pine nuts
1/2 cup olive oil
Salt and pepper to taste

Oregano Pesto
1/2 cup oregano leaves
1 to 1-1/2 cup parsley leaves
2 large garlic cloves
1/2 grated Parmesan cheese
1/2 cup walnuts or pine nuts
1/2 cup olive oil

For Venison
Whisk the pestos, rosemary, chili peppers, mince onion, oils and lemon juice until blended. Add venison, mix, make sure all the venison is coated. Marinate for 1 to 2 hours in refrigerator. Bring to room temperature before grilling. Skewer the venison, peppers, onions, and mushrooms onto wooden skewers leaving a little space between each piece.

Grill on hot gas or charcoal grill about 4 to 5 inches from heat. Grill until meat is medium-rare and veggies are just beginning to char. Brush with marinade and serve.

For Pesto's
Put all ingredients except olive oil into food processor. Process to mix and chop ingredients. With the machine running, slowing add oil until mixture is smooth. (Extra oil might need to be added to make the mixture smooth and creamy). Freeze the remaining pesto in muffin tins lined with plastic wrap in 1 or 2 tablespoon amounts. This way when you make the recipe again you have pre-measured amounts.

Chapter 6

Venison Soups & Stews

Mike's Venison Vegetable Soup

Mike Haas, OH

1 pound ground venison (any ground game meat)
3 cans mixed vegetables
2 cans french-style green beans
1 can cut green beans
1 can V8 juice
1 small Vidalia (sweet) onion, chopped
3 cans stewed tomatoes
2 beef bouillon cubes
1 teaspoon garlic powder
1/2 cup ketchup

In your cooking pot, fry the ground meat, adding the chopped onions. When onions are done, add all the other ingredients and mix. If you drain the vegetables, be sure to add enough water to cover the ingredients. Bring to a boil, then allow to simmer for 45 minutes. Bring to a boil then allow to simmer for 45 minutes, occasionally stirring. For a little more punch on a cold day, you can add 1 tablespoon of chile powder and 2 cans of black beans.

Taco Bean Soup

Jim Lazenby, NC

1 pound deer burger
1 chopped medium onion
1 package ranch dressing
1 package taco seasoning mix
1 cup warm water
2 cans of Rotel

2 cans drained pinto beans
1 can drained black beans
1 can of cream style corn
Sour cream
Taco style cheese

Brown the meat and drain and add onion. Put it in a slow cooker and add everything except the sour cream and cheese. Cook on med heat for one hour, then serve with sour cream and cheese. Corn bread also goes great with it.

Deer Soup

Bob Salyers, OH

1 pound of ground deer
1 pound of backstraps cut in chunks
2 cans of kernel corn
2 cans of mushrooms

2 cans of sliced potatoes
1 can of green beans
1 jar of V8 juice
1 jar of mild salsa

Brown the deer burger and then the backstraps. Put it in a large pan with the tomato juice/salsa. Add the corn, potatoes, green beans and mushrooms and bring to a boil for about 10 minutes. Cover and simmer, then serve.

Wilderness Cinnamon Jerky Noodle Soup

Doug Thalacker, IN   *Serves 2*

1/4 cup venison or other
   wild game jerky
1 cup noodles
2 packets soy sauce
1 teaspoon cinnamon
1/2 teaspoon onion flakes

1/2 teaspoon garlic powder
1/4 teaspoon ground ginger
1/4 teaspoon pepper flakes (optional)
1 teaspoon dry cilantro
1/4 to 1/3 cup dried vegetables

At Home: Mix all dry ingredients except the jerky and noodles in a zip-locking bag. Carry jerky and noodles in a separate bag.

At camp: Add noodle/jerky mix to 2 cups boiling water. Cook until meat is tender and noodles are soft. Add dry ingredients and soy sauce. Soup will thicken as it sits.

Pop's Venison Stew

Robert Tanner, GA

3 cups venison, cut into 1-inch cubes
3 cups vegetables (potatoes, carrots and celery)
1 clove garlic, minced
1 medium onion
3 cups water or broth
2 tablespoons tomato paste
1-ounce hot sauce
Salt and pepper to taste

Brown the venison in a cast iron skillet. Then combine all the ingredients in a crock pot. Turn on low and let cook for at least 6 hours. Do not stir. Serve hot, with corn bread if desired.

Venison Vegetable Soup

Clay Whittaker, IN

1 tablespoon vegetable oil
1 pound venison, cut into cubes
1 cup diced onion
1 (16 ounce) package frozen mixed vegetables
2 (14.5 ounce) cans peeled and diced tomatoes with juice
3 cups potatoes, peeled and cubed
4 cups water
1 tablespoon white sugar
2 teaspoons beef bouillon granules
1 teaspoon salt
1/2 teaspoon ground black pepper
1/2 teaspoon garlic powder
1/4 teaspoon hot pepper sauce

Heat oil in a stock pot or Dutch oven over medium high heat. Brown the venison in the hot oil. Add onion, cover pot and simmer over medium heat for 10 minutes, or until onions are translucent.

Stir the mixed vegetables, tomatoes and potatoes. Combine the water, sugar and bouillon, stir into the soup. Season with salt, pepper, garlic powder and hot pepper sauce. Cover and simmer for at least one hour, or until the meat is tender.

Venison Stew

Jackie Jaggers, KY

2 pounds ground venison (browned)
1 can whole kernel corn
1 can cream style corn
1 24-ounce can tomato puree
3 stalks of celery, chopped
1 tablespoon cumin

Bring corn, tomato puree and celery to a boil. Let simmer 30 minutes. Take off heat and add the browned venison and cumin. Let it simmer another 30 minutes over low heat.

Deer Camp Stew

Jason Houser, IL

4 pounds stew or neck meat, cut into 1-inch cubes
3 tablespoons flour
3 tablespoons cooking oil
10 cups water
1-1/2 teaspoons granulated garlic
3 tablespoons soy sauce
2 packages Au jus mix
2 large onions, quartered and thickly sliced
4 large potatoes, peeled and 1-inch cubed
5 large carrots, washed and 1/2-inch sliced
2 large turnips, peeled and 1-inch cubed
1 medium green cabbage, cored and coarsely sliced
4 stalks celery, 1/2-inch pieces
2 (16-ounce) cans diced tomatoes
1 (6-ounce) can green peas
1 (6-ounce) can corn
1 (6-ounce) can cut green beans
1 (6-ounce) can sliced mushrooms
Salt and pepper

Add 10 cups water to a very large pot and place over high heat. Season the cubed meat well with salt, pepper and granulated garlic. Dust and lightly coat the meat with flour. Lightly brown all the meat in small batches in a frying pan with some of the cooking oil. Dump each batch into the stew pot after browning. Add the remaining granulated garlic, soy sauce, and one package of the au jus mix to the stew pot. Add onion, potatoes, carrots, turnips and celery. Bring the pot to a boil then reduce heat to maintain a good simmer. Allow to simmer 30 minutes, Then add canned tomatoes, peas, corn and green beans, including the juices and mushrooms with juices. Simmer for another hour, stirring frequently to prevent sticking and burning. Taste. If needed add the second au jus mix package and mix well. Stir in sliced cabbage. Simmer for another 30 to 60 minutes or until the cabbage is fully cooked. Serve. Refrigerate leftovers for the next night.

Deer Steak Stew

Carmela Collins, PA

Venison steak
Cream of mushroom soup
Potatoes
Peppers

Onions
Carrots
Celery

Sear the deer steak in hot oil for about 30 seconds on each side. In crock pot add cream of mushroom soup, potatoes, peppers, onions, carrots, celery and the whole deer steak. Let cook on high for about 6 hours. Turn down to low for another 6 hours. Your steak will fall apart.

Venison and Wild Mushroom Stew

Andrew Roney, WA

6 strips bacon, cut into 1/2-inch pieces
2 pounds venison shoulder, excess fat removed, cut into 1-inch cubes
Salt and pepper
1/4 cup flour
1/4 cup vegetable oil
1 cup dry red wine
1 large onion, diced
1 large carrot, peeled and diced
2 ribs celery, diced
1 large parsnip, peeled and diced

1 leek, white only, diced
2 teaspoons minced garlic
1 pound mixed wild mushrooms (wood ear, chanterelle, morel, or shiitake)
1 12-ounce can dark beer
2-1/2 quarts veal or beef stock
2 tablespoons Worcestershire sauce
6 sprigs fresh thyme
1 teaspoon allspice
3 bay leaves
2 tablespoons tomato paste
4 large red potatoes, 1/2-inch diced

In a large stockpot cook the bacon over high heat until crispy. Remove the bacon from the pan and drain. Season the venison with salt and pepper, and then lightly dust with flour. Add the oil to the pot and sear the venison on all sides over medium high heat. Remove the meat from the pot and add any remaining flour, stirring constantly. Deglaze the pot with the red wine, scraping with a wooden spoon. Add the onions and cook over medium high heat until translucent, about 3 minutes. Add the carrots, celery and parsnips and saute for 2 minutes, then add the leeks and garlic and cook for 2 minutes. Add the mushrooms to the pot and cook until they release their moisture, about 5 to 7 minutes. Add the beer and scrape to remove any browned bits from the bottom of the pan, then add the veal stock, Worcestershire sauce, thyme, allspice, bay leaves and tomato paste. Boil, then reduce heat to a simmer. Cook until meat is tender, about 1-1/2 hours. Add potatoes and continue cooking until they are cooked through, about 20 to 30 minutes.

Big Buck Rub Stew

William Moeller, MO

1 pound chunked deer meat
1 whole onion
1 tablespoon salt
2 tablespoons pepper
1 tablespoon Worcestershire sauce

2 tablespoons hot sauce
5 to 6 large potatoes, cut in 1-inch chunks
One packet onion soup mix
5 to 6 chopped whole carrots

Place chunked deer meat in crock pot. Cover meat with onion soup mix, salt and pepper, and add enough water to approximately 1 inch in bottom of pot. Add Worcestershire sauce and hot sauce to water. Add carrots and potatoes. Slow cook 6 to 8 hours on low heat.

Venison and Wild Rice Stew

Bryan Thurm, IA

3-1/2 pounds venison, cut in 2-inch cubes
2 quarts water
2 onions, peeled and quartered

2 teaspoons salt
1/8 teaspoon pepper
1-1/2 cups wild rice

Place venison, water, and onions in a large, heavy kettle. Simmer uncovered for 3 hours. Mix in salt, pepper, and wild rice. Cover and simmer for 20 minutes. Uncover and simmer for 20 minutes until rice is tender and most of the liquid is absorbed. Then it's time to feast!

Buckeroo Stew

Nathan Waters, OH

1 pound venison, cut into smaller chunks
1 sweet yellow onion, chopped into large pieces
6 cloves of garlic, chopped
1 tablespoon olive oil or butter if you want it to be extra delicious
1 can diced tomatoes
1-2 teaspoons dried thyme
Salt and pepper to taste
2 bay leaves
6 cups of beef stock
1 cup diced carrots
1 cup diced celery
2 cups diced baby red potatoes (skin on)

Place all the ingredients in a crock pot and heat on high until it reaches a good simmer. Then turn it to low and leave it to simmer all day long. Serve with fresh biscuits, rolls or corn bread.

Venison Barley-Brussel Sprout Stew

Debra Sluis, MN

3 or 4 cups cubed venison
Water to cover the ingredients
1 large onion
Salt & pepper

2 teaspoons thyme
1 pound brussels sprouts
1 cup pearled barley
2 tablespoons oil

Brown the meat and the onion in the oil. Then, combine all the rest of the ingredients in a stockpot or crock pot and simmer for at least 4 hours.

Sweet and Sour Deer Stew

David Henry, PA

1-1/2 pounds of venison cut into 1-inch cubes
2 tablespoons cooking oil
2 medium carrots, shredded
2 medium onions, sliced
1 8-ounce can of tomato sauce
1/2 cup water
Cooked noodles

1/4 cup packed brown sugar
1/4 cup vinegar
1 tablespoon Worcestershire sauce
1 teaspoon salt
1 tablespoon water
2 teaspoons cornstarch

Brown the meat, half at a time, in a 3-quart saucepan. In the same pan, combine the meat, carrot, onion, tomato sauce, 1/2 cup water, brown sugar, vinegar, Worcestershire sauce and salt. Cover and cook over low heat until the meat is tender, about 1-1/2 hours. Blend 1 tablespoon water with cornstarch and add to stew. Serve over hot noodles.

Crock Pot Stew

Christy Jurasek, TX

1/2 cup diced celery
1/2 cup diced yellow onion
1/4 diced shallots w/green tops
2 garlic gloves, ran thru press
1 can Rotel tomatoes
1 teaspoon chicken base or 1 bullion cube
2 teaspoons seasoned salt
1/2 teaspoon paprika (smoked is best)
1 tablespoon chili powder
1-1/2 pounds cubed beef (wild pork or venison)

Combine all the ingredients in slow cooker and add enough water to bring near the top of cooker. Set on hi heat for 6 to 8 hours. The meat should be so soft it cuts with the side of a fork. Serve by the bowl, topped with your favorite toppings. Shredded cheese, croutons, oyster crackers or even club cracker are a few suggestions.

Venison Stew

Jeffrey Lucowitz, VA

2 to 3 pounds of venison cubes
1 tablespoon salt
2 tablespoons of Worcestershire sauce
2 tablespoons liquid smoke
4 medium red potatoes, cubed
6 medium carrots, chopped

4 celery stalks, chopped
2 teaspoons minced garlic
4 tablespoons olive oil
1 packet onion soup mix
6 cups of water
3 tablespoons of cornstarch

Rinse venison and pat dry. Heat oil in dutch oven to medium high, rub meat with salt, liquid smoke, and Worcestershire sauce. Brown the meat until the liquid is absorbed, add water, soup mix, and garlic and let simmer for 1.5 hours. Add potatoes, carrots, and celery; simmer until tender. Prior to serving, add remaining liquid smoke and corn starch by stirring them into the broth and allow to thicken.

Chapter 7

Venison Main Dishes

Deer Parmesan

Daniel Jones, MO

1 venison tenderloin
Bread crumbs
Egg wash

1 can of crushed tomatoes
Parmesan or mozzarella cheese
Olive oil

   Slice the tenderloin and pound it thin. Place it in egg wash and bread crumbs then fry in skillet with olive oil until brown place in oven cover with crushed tomatoes and cheese melt until desired color and serve.

Home-Style Venison Stroganoff

Alan Reisdorph, LA

1 pound venison, cut into cubes
Salt and pepper to taste
Garlic powder to taste
1 onion, chopped
1 clove garlic, chopped
2 (10.75 ounce) cans condensed cream of mushroom soup
1 (16 ounce) package frozen egg noodles
1 (8 ounce) container sour cream
2 cups of wild rice or long grain rice

Season venison with salt, pepper and garlic powder to taste. Saute onion a garlic in a large skillet with olive oil; when soft, add venison and brown. Drain when venison is no longer pink and add soup. Reduce heat to low and simmer. Meanwhile, bring a large pot of lightly salted water to a boil. Add noodles and cook for 8 to 10 minutes or until al dente; drain. In another small pan boil rice until tender, cover with lid and cool. When noodles are almost done cooking, stir in sour cream and meat. Serve over rice and enjoy.

Tenderloin Biscuits

Sherri Letner, TN

2 pounds tenderloin, cut 1/2-inch thick 1 cup milk
2 cups flour (with a dash of salt) 2 cups oil
2 eggs Biscuits

Make an egg wash with milk and eggs. Roll the tenderloin steaks in the flour after dipping them in egg wash. Pan fry. Pop biscuits out of oven and serve together. Add fried eggs for a great breakfast.

Fajitas ala Venison

Moises Campos, CA

2 teaspoons seasoned salt
1/4 teaspoon garlic salt
1/2 teaspoon black pepper
1/2 teaspoon cayenne pepper
1 teaspoon dried oregano
1-1/2 pounds venison, cut into 2-inch strips
4 tablespoons vegetable oil
1 medium red bell pepper, cut into 2-inch strips
1 medium yellow bell pepper, cut into 2-inch strips
1 medium onion, cut into 1/2-inch wedges
12 fajita size flour tortillas, warmed

Combine seasoned salt, garlic salt, black pepper, cayenne pepper, and oregano to make the fajita seasoning. Sprinkle two teaspoons of the seasoning over the sliced venison. Mix well, cover, and refrigerate for 30 minutes. Heat 2 tablespoons of oil in a heavy frying pan. Cook bell peppers and onion until starting to soften, then remove. Pour in remaining oil, then cook venison until browned. Return pepper mixture to the pan, season with remaining fajita seasoning, and reheat. Served with the warmed tortillas.

Cinnamon Venison

Theodore O'Donnell, VA

Cubed venison
1 stick real butter
Cinnamon

Cut venison into chunks 2 inches long by 1 inch tall and no more than 1/2 inch thick. In a cast iron skillet, melt lots of butter and use as much cinnamon as you can handle. Cook the venison in the mix for several minutes, then turn and cook a few more minutes. Don't overdo it. The butter and spice will make a gravy.

Venison Goulash

John Sterba, PA

2 pounds venison stew meat
6 medium potatoes
4 carrots
2 sticks celery
4 cloves garlic

1 medium onion
Salt & pepper
Parsley flakes
2 quarts stewed tomatoes
1 quart water

In a large pot brown meat, add stewed tomatoes. Slice potatoes, carrots, celery, onions and garlic. Add them in pot. Salt and pepper to taste. Sprinkle in parsley flakes, add water, stir. Cook on medium heat until carrots and potatoes are done.

Rib-Stickin' Cheesy Venison and Noodles

Thomas Walker, MI

1 pound venison stew meat
1/2 medium onion
2 tablespoons vegetable oil
1 12-ounce can of mushrooms

1 14-ounce can green beans (optional)
8 ounces uncooked noodles
1 16-ounce pkg Velveta cheese, cut into chunks
Salt or season to taste

Brown venison and onions in vegetable oil in a frying pan. Add mushrooms to heat through. Drain excess oil if any. Salt to taste. Boil noodles in saucepan according to package directions. Drain. Combine meat mixture, green beans (if using), noodles and Velveta chunks in pan and stir over low heat until cheese is melted.

Venison Parm

Bruce Green, NJ

1 venison tenderloin,
    cut into 1/2-inch thick medallions
2 eggs beaten
2 cups Italian bread crumbs
1/2 teaspoon garlic powder

2 packages shredded mozzarella
1 26-ounce jar spaghetti sauce
2 tablespoons olive oil
1/2 teaspoon Italian seasoning

Pound venison tenderloins into 1/4-inch thick pieces. Add garlic powder to bread crumbs and mix thoroughly. Dredge venison in beaten eggs, then coat each side with bread crumb mixture. Add olive oil to large frying pan and heat on medium heat. Fry coated venison browning both sides. Coat bottom of 9-inch deep dish casserole with some of the tomato sauce. Layer venison and coat with some of the tomato sauce. Top sauce with the mozzarella cheese. Repeat for three or four layers with venison, sauce and cheese. Sprinkle top of last layer of cheese with Italian seasoning. Bake uncovered at 350 degrees for 1/2 hour. Serve with crusty Italian bread, salad and a bottle of Chianti.

Tony's Tasty Venison

Anthony Thompson, WV

1 pound thinly sliced venison backstrap
Soy sauce
1 large onion
1 large green pepper
1 portobello mushroom

Black pepper
Lemon pepper
Butter
White and wild rice

Saute venison in large bowl with soy sauce, lemon pepper, and black pepper overnight. In a hot frying pan melt 1/2 stick butter, add venison searing one side then turn meat over, turn heat down to medium and add sliced onion, sliced green pepper, and sliced mushrooms. Fry until the meat is just done do not over cook so the vegetables do not get too soft. Serve over cooked white and wild rice.

Teriyaki Loin Chops

Glen Healey, MO

6 loin chops 1 to 2-inch thick [what ever type venison you have on hand]
1 cup Kikkoman's teriyaki
1/2 cup red wine
1 cup pineapple juice

1/3 cup brown sugar
3 cloves garlic
1 tablespoon fresh cracked black pepper

Loin chops should be trimmed no tendons or silver skin in a mixing bowl combine all liquid ingredients peel and crush garlic add garlic brown sugar and pepper to liquid and mix well place chops in gallon size freezer bag add liquid seal and shake place in fridge for at least 48 hours turn and shake bag several times during the 48 hours remove chops from marinade and let them come up to room temperature grill over hot coals for 5 minutes per side you want medium rare do not over cook let chops rest for 5-8 minutes and serve foiled potatoes with onions and cooked cabbage make great sides.

Venison Philly Steak Sandwich

Al Higgins, MD

Venison steak
Sliced American cheese
1 onion
1 green pepper

Crusty roll
Olive oil
Butter

Slice the steak as thin as possible (it helps if it is still partially frozen).Pour 2 tablespoons of oil in a frying pan. While waiting for it to heat up saute the onion and pepper in 1 tablespoon of olive oil and 1 tablespoon of butter. Toast the rolls. When the pan gets hot - high heat - place steak slices in the pan and immediately begin to stir the meat as it cook. As soon as the meat begins to brown drop the cheese into the pan and continue stirring until the cheese has completely melted and produced a nice, thick sauce. Serve on a toasted roll, topped with the onions and peppers and serve with plenty of napkins.

Venison Yumbo

Mark O'Connor, NY

1 pound venison hamburger
2 cups rice
2 cans diced tomatoes
1 large white onion
1 large green pepper

1 can of sliced mushrooms
Salt and pepper
Garlic
Cajun seasoning
Grated cheese

Brown the venison in frying pan adding salt pepper garlic to you're taste. Then, put it in a pot. Dice the onions peppers mushrooms and put them in a frying pan to cook until the onions and peppers are tender. Add to venison in pot. In another pot, boil rice until tender. Add diced tomatoes to venison pot. After that is all warm, add the rice, mixing it all together.

You may have to add some tomato paste if looks dry. Start adding Cajun seasoning to the pot until the mix is at your desired spicyness. Sprinkle grated cheese over the top as much as you want, then put it in oven until the cheese melts and is golden brown. Serve warm and enjoy.

Venison Schnitzel

Jesus Armas Jr., FL

2 pounds venison tenderloin
1/4 cup vegetable oil
2 teaspoons bacon drippings
3/4 cup all-purpose flour
1 teaspoon salt
1/4 teaspoon freshly ground black pepper
1 egg, lightly beaten
2 tablespoons milk
1 cup dry bread crumbs
1/2 cup crushed buttery round cracker crumbs
2 tablespoons lemon juice

Cut tenderloin into 1/2 inch steaks. Slice each steak in half horizontally, from the smallest toward the largest side, until there is only a very small section keeping the two halves connected. Slice a few small scores on the outer edges of each steak to prevent them from curling up when frying. Preheat oil and bacon drippings in a large heavy skillet over medium high heat. In a large shallow dish, combine flour, salt and pepper. In a separate shallow bowl, beat together egg and milk. In another shallow dish, combine bread crumbs and cracker crumbs. Dredge the steaks in the seasoned flour, and using a meat mallet, pound them down to just slightly less than their 1/4 inch thickness. Dip the steaks in the egg mixture, then coat each steak on both sides with the crumbs. Set aside on a clean plate. When all steaks are evenly coated, place prepared steaks gently in a single layer into the hot oil. Fry steaks for 2 to 3 minutes on each side, or until golden brown. Drain on paper towels. Sprinkle each steak lightly with lemon juice.

Chapter 8

Venison BBQ & Ribs

Deer Barbecue

Jim Humphrey, IN

2 deer roasts
1 can mushrooms
1 bell pepper
1 onion
Brown sugar
Barbecue sauce of your choice

Cook deer roasts either in a slow cooker or pressure cooker. When the deer meat is done, shred it and put it in a slow cooker. Chop up the bell pepper and onion, then add to the deer meat. Drain the mushrooms before adding. When you have added your desired Barbecue sauce, finish by sprinkling brown sugar on top of your mixture. Put the lid on and cook on low to medium heat until green pepper and onions are tender.

Jerry's Pulled Venison Tenderloin

Jerome Kryspin, DE

2 pounds venison tenderloin
1 quart of apple cider
Barbecue sauce of choice

   Place venison tenderloin in crock pot on low. Pour apple cider over tenderloin and cook for 8 hours. Remove tenderloin and place on cutting board. Use two forks to pull apart. Place pulled meat back in crock pot for 45 minutes after covering with favorite barbecue sauce.
   Enjoy!

Korean-Style Venison Barbecue Over Coconut Rice

Bob Martin, AK

1 pound thinly sliced venison steak (sirloin)
5 tablespoons brown sugar
1/2 cup soy sauce
6 cloves garlic, grated
1/4 teaspoon salt
5 tablespoons Mirin (sweet sake, optional)
2 tablespoons toasted sesame oil
1 teaspoon Tabasco sauce
2 tablespoons toasted sesame seeds
1 cup green onions, split
2 cups thinly sliced carrots
1 hibachi grill or similar small grill

Coconut-Sesame Jasmine Rice:
2 cups jasmine rice
2-ounces coconut syrup
6 ounces coconut milk
1 cup water
1 tablespoon butter
1 teaspoon toasted sesame oil

   Mix all ingredients except carrots. Marinate in refrigerator for at least 2 hours; however, overnight is the best. Place slices of venison on the grill rack and cook on high for 7 minutes, 31/2 minutes on each side basting strips with extra marinate. Place marinated carrots around the venison and cook. You will have to cook the venison in two different shifts if using small grill.

Coconut-Sesame Jasmine Rice:
    In a 6 cup pot, place water, coconut syrup, and sesame oil in pot set on high till it starts bubbling. Place Jasmine rice in liquid and stir till rice starts to boil then turn down the heat to simmer for approximately 15 to 20 minutes or until rice is al dente.

    Serve over coconut sesame Jasmine rice and enjoy

BBQ Bacon-Wrapped Grilled Venison-Stuffed Jalapeño

Matthew Smith, PA

Venison choice cuts, slice into bite size pieces
Large jalapeño peppers
Cream cheese
Onion slices
Green pepper, cut into strips
Maple-flavored bacon
Your favorite barbecue sauce
Toothpicks

    Season the venison to taste with your favorite seasonings. Remove the tips and stems from the jalapeños. Slice lengthwise in half and remove the seeds. Spread some cream cheese into each pepper half. Insert one piece of venison into the pepper. Top with a slice of onion and green pepper. Wrap with a slice of bacon and secure with toothpicks. Repeat with the rest of the ingredients. Grill over medium heat. When the bacon is done, venison should be done. Baste with barbecue sauce when just about done.

Bourbon BBQ

Jason Houser, IL

1 to 2 pound venison roast,
    cut into thin slices
2 tablespoons liquid smoke
1/4 cup brown sugar
1 tablespoon lemon juice

1-1/2 cups water
2/3 cup soy sauce
1/2 cup bourbon (whiskey)
1 teaspoon Worcestershire sauce

Place liquid smoke, brown sugar, lemon juice, water, soy sauce, whiskey and Worcestershire sauce into a self-sealing plastic bag. Add the sliced roast and marinate for 1 hour. Pour meat and marinade into a hot frying pan with about 2 tablespoons cooking oil and cook until meat is pink in the middle, about 5 minutes.

BBQ Venison Roast

Wil Rhodes, GA

1 or 2 deer roasts (depending on size)
1 sweet onion, peeled and finely chopped
1 whole clove of fresh garlic, peeled and chopped/sliced
4 sticks (1 pound) unsalted butter, at room temperature
1 package (1 pound) bacon
Cracked pepper
Sea salt
Barbecue sauce (I recommend Cattlemen's Smokehouse BBQ)

Preheat oven to 300 F. Place roasts in a traditional roasting pan. Rub roast(s) down with the cracked pepper and sea salt. Rub 3 sticks of room temperature butter all over the roast(s). Place remaining stick of butter if a sauce pan over medium heat. Add garlic and onions to butter in sauce pan. Saute garlic and onions in butter until garlic just starts to get soft. Remove from heat. Slowly pour over roast(s). Remove bacon from package. Piece by piece, drape bacon evenly over the roast(s) until it is completely covered (If you have any extra bacon leftover, it's okay to put it directly on top of the other bacon). Cover top of the pan with aluminum foil. Place in the preheated oven for 6-8 hours. Remove the pan and baste the roasts every 45 minutes or so. You'll know it's done when it literally falls apart when touched with a fork or other utensil. Remove from oven and remove foil. Carefully peel off and discard bacon (if any roast is stuck to the bacon, please try and save it because it will be so yummy that you don't want to waste it). Using a large serving fork and a slotted spoon, move the roast to a large dish (glass bowl or casserole dish) and pull it apart into shreds. You might have to fish out some pieces of roast from the juices in the bottom using the slotted spoon. Once all the roast is in the large dish, take a large spoon and pour 1-2 spoonfuls of the drippings over the roast shreds and mix around with the spoon. While the roast is still hot, pour in your Cattlemen's Smokehouse BBQ sauce. Stir until coated. Serve on garlic toast or sesame seed buns or just eat it with a fork.

Pulled Venison

David Mahosky, CA

3-4 pounds of any cuts of venison
1 package of McCormick's slow cookers
   BBQ pulled pork seasoning mix
1/2 cup ketchup
1/2 cup brown sugar

1/3 cup cider vinegar
1/4 cup molasses
2 large apples (not granny smith)
Large buns/rolls

    Quarter and deseed the apples, Put half of them in the bottom of a crock pot (no need to peel them). Cut the venison to fit in the crock pot. Mix ketchup, brown sugar, cider vinegar, molasses and McCormick seasoning. Put venison in crock pot and pour mixture over top of venison. Add remaining apples just inside of the top of mixture. Cook on low for 8 hours. When done, pull apart venison and mix well with sauce in crock pot. Apples will be incorporated. Serve on buns or rolls.

Barbecue Venison

German Rojas, VA

2 pounds of any cut of venison, no fat
1 tablespoon of ginger

1 tablespoon lemon juice
Seasoned salt

    Slow cook in a crock pot for 8 hours. Remove and shred meat. Place back in crock pot, and add you favorite bottle of BBQ sauce. Cook on low for 1 hour. Remove from heat, and serve with potato rolls and a favorite side dish.

Shredded Venison

Justin Lehto, MI

2 venison roasts
1 large onion
1 bottle ketchup

1 cup brown sugar
2 tablespoons liquid smoke

Cook the venison and onion for about 7 or 8 hours in a crock pot. Shred the meat with two forks. Return the meat to the crock pot and add the remaining ingredients. Mix and let cook for about 20 minutes. Serve on a hard roll or bun of your choice. Or, serve over some thick noodles.

Pistachio-Crusted Rack of Venison

Andrew Roney, WA

2 racks venison (4 bones each)
4 tablespoons olive oil
1/2 cup toasted and ground pistachios
1/2 cup bread crumbs
1/3 cup Dijon mustard
2-1/2 tablespoons paprika
2 tablespoons salt

2 tablespoons garlic powder
1 tablespoon black pepper
1 tablespoon onion powder
1 tablespoon cayenne pepper
1 tablespoon dried oregano
1 tablespoon dried thyme

Cranberry, Black Pepper, Sage Reduction:
2 teaspoons olive oil
1 tablespoon minced shallots
1/2 teaspoon minced garlic
1/2 cup dry red wine
2 teaspoons chopped fresh sage leaves
2 teaspoons cold unsalted butter

1/4 cup dried cranberries
1-1/2 cups veal stock
1/4 teaspoon kosher salt
1/4 teaspoon freshly ground black
    pepper

Preheat the oven to 450 degrees F. Mix 2 tablespoons of salt, garlic powder, and paprika, and then 1 Tablespoon of , black pepper, onion powder, cayenne pepper, dried oregano, and dried thyme, in a small bowl and then season the venison with half the mixture. Reserve other half for further use.

Place a 12-inch skillet over medium-high heat. Add 2 tablespoons of the olive oil to the pan and once the pan is hot, sear the venison on the bone side for 1 minute. Using tongs, turn the racks and sear on each of the other sides, until nicely browned on all sides. Remove racks from the pan and allow to cool completely.

In a medium bowl combine the pistachios, bread crumbs, 1/2 teaspoon of seasoning mix and 2 tablespoons of olive oil. Toss well.

Once the ribs are cool enough to handle, rub the racks with the mustard, using about 1 1/2 tablespoons of mustard per rack. Dredge each rack into the bread crumb mixture to evenly coat. Turn down the oven temperature to 400 degrees F. Place the racks in a skillet and roast in the oven 15 to 20 minutes or an instant read thermometer inserted into its center registers 140 degrees F for medium-rare.

Cranberry, Black Pepper, Sage Reduction:

Place a 10-inch skillet over medium heat and add the olive oil. Once the oil is hot, add the shallots and garlic. Cook, stirring often, until the shallots are almost clear, about 1 minute. Deglaze the pan with the red wine and raise the heat to medium-high. Add the sage and cherries and continue to cook until the wine is reduced to about 2 tablespoons, about 3 minutes. Add the stock to the pan and bring to a boil, reduce to a simmer, and cook until reduced to 1 cup, about 10 minutes. Season with salt and black pepper and mix in the cold butter. Serve immediately or cover to keep warm until ready to serve.

Chapter 9

Venison Chili

Good Old Reliable

Carl Day, OH

2 pounds ground venison
1 large onion
3 large cans Campbell's tomato soup
2 cans kidney beans

1 can of Bush's chili beans (medium)
1 small can of mushroom pieces
2 tablespoons of Chugwater chili mix

Fry the ground venison and chopped onion. Drain. Add with all the other ingredients into a crock pot and simmer for a few hours. I like to serve it with shredded cheese and nachos.

Venison Fire Chili

Rick Fitzpatrick, MI

2 pounds venison	Two 15.5 ounce cans spicy kidney beans
Salt and pepper	One 15.5 ounce can northern white beans
Cayenne pepper	1/4 to 1/3 cup chopped onions
1/4 to 1/2 pounds ground pepperoni	3-5 cloves of garlic chopped
Chilli powder	1-2 cap fulls of olive oil
Three 28-ounce cans tomato puree plus 1-2 6 ounce cans	

Place the onion, garlic and olive oil into a hot frying pan, begin browning then add venison browning with salt, pepper, chill powder. After browning add the pepperoni and tomato paste, spice to taste with cayenne, salt pepper, chilli powder, approximately 5 - 10 minutes on medium heat. Once this is done drain any excess water, if any and place in to a sauce pot adding the tomato puree, beans, cover bring to a slow boil, for 30 minutes, reduce heat and simmer for 2 - 4 hours depending on serving time.

Serve in either bread bowls or regular bowls garnish with green onion, shredded cheddar cheese and dollop of sour cream.

Best Chili

Brian Gottschall, TN

1 pound dry kidney beans	28-ounce can tomatoes, diced
1 pound ground venison	1 large onion, diced
1 pound venison stew meat, in 1/2-inch chunks	1 green pepper, diced
	1 large green chili pepper, diced
2 tablespoons oil	1/4 teaspoon cumin
2 cloves garlic, minced	2 tablespoons parsley, chopped
3 teaspoons chili powder	1/4 cup masa flour or all purpose flour
1 teaspoon salt	Water
1/2 teaspoon pepper	

Place beans in a large soup kettle. Add 2 quarts water and 2 tsp salt; cover the pot and bring to a boil. Boil gently for about 2 hours, until beans are tender. Brown meat in a large skillet containing oil and garlic. Add chili powder, salt and pepper. Cover and saute for an hour. Drain the beans and add 1½ quarts water, tomatoes, onion, peppers, cumin and parsley. Simmer for an hour, then add meat mixture. Stir masa flour into ½ cup water to form a paste and blend into chili to thicken. Simmer for about half an hour, adjust the seasonings and serve.

Hunting Chili

Lester Legan, CA

1 pound ground venison
1 pound of chopped venison
1 large red onion, chopped
2 red bell peppers, chopped
2 orange bell peppers, chopped
2 yellow bell peppers, chopped
6 fresh jalapeño peppers, chopped
2 fresh Habanero peppers, finely chopped
1 clove garlic, crushed

1 large can of stewed tomatoes
(I prefer the Mexican style seasoned)
2 small cans of tomato paste
1 large can black beans
1 large can red kidney beans
1 large can of sweet white corn
1 teaspoon of ground sage
4 teaspoons of Creole Seasoning
Olive oil (extra virgin)

Saute the onions and garlic till translucent and starting to caramelize put in large pot or slow cooker, in the same pan that you did onions cook your ground venison adding some extra virgin olive oil when well cooked add to pot, then brown your chopped venison in the same pan add olive oil cook quickly so as to only brown the meat, add the slow cooker. Now add all the other ingredients to the pot or slow cooker add about 4 or 5 cups of water, set heat at medium cook for 2 hours or on low heat for 3 hours.

Serve with fresh corn bread or flour tortillas.

Roland and Dawn Gagnon's Venison Chili

Roland Gagnon, RI

2 teaspoons vegetable oil
2 pounds ground venison
1 pound venison sausage
1 red onion, diced
2 stalks celery, diced
4 large jalapeño peppers, diced or minced
1 each red and green pepper, diced
Two 15 1/2-ounce cans of kidney beans
One 16-ounce can of baked beans (not tomato based)
Two 14-ounce cans of diced tomatoes
One 6-ounce can of tomato paste
1 cup red wine
1/4 cup Worcestershire sauce
2 tablespoons chili powder
2 teaspoons cumin
1 teaspoon coriander

1 tablespoon dried oregano
4 bay leaves
1/2 teaspoon allspice

On medium high heat, brown meat in 1 lb batches, unless you have a big enough skillet or stockpot. Drain and keep warm. In the same skillet or stockpot, cook onion, celery, carrots and jalapenos in vegetable oil until onion is clear. Add the meat and the rest of the ingredients. Bring to a slight boil on medium high heat, stirring occasionally. Reduce heat and simmer uncovered for about an hour. Can be made in a 6 quart or larger crock pot. After cooking meat and vegetables mix, all the ingredients in a crock pot and cook 8 hours on high or 4 hours on low.

Venison Chili

William McCorquodale, NC

2 pounds venison
1/4 pound thick cut bacon, diced
2 medium yellow onions, diced
1 medium red onion, diced
2 jalapeño chili peppers, seeded and diced
1 red pepper, seeded and diced
1 yellow pepper, seeded and diced
1 green pepper, seeded and diced
1/4 of an 8-ounce can of chipotle chili
    peppers, seeded and finely chopped
3 minced garlic cloves
1/4 cup of balsamic vinegar
4 tablespoons of chili powder

1 tablespoon paprika
1 tablespoon cumin
1 tablespoon salt
1 tablespoon black pepper
1 tablespoon cinnamon
1/4 cup of honey
1 tablespoon molasses
1 bottle of Guinness or other stout beer
1/2 cup red wine
1 can of whole plum tomatoes
1 can of crushed tomatoes
2 cans of black beans

In a large pan, saute venison until just cooked. Drain and set aside. Cook in batches if necessary to keep from crowding in the pan. In a large heavy bottomed pot, saute bacon over medium heat until it's brown and has given up its fat. Remove and set aside. Saute onions and peppers in the bacon fat, stirring frequently, until soft, about 5 minutes. Add garlic and vinegar and cook for 2 minutes. Add chili powder, paprika, cumin, salt, pepper, cinnamon and cook, stirring often, for about 3 minutes. Add venison and bacon. Stir well and cook for 1 minute. Add honey, molasses, beer, wine and tomatoes. Mix well, bring to a boil, and reduce heat to low. Cook at a slow simmer, uncovered, for an hour and stir frequently. Taste and adjust seasoning. Add beans and cook for another hour. Garnish with chopped cilantro (optional).

Venison Ranch Chili

Dean Breitenfeldt, WI

1 pound venison meat
1/2 cup chopped onion
2 teaspoons cooking oil
3 tablespoons chili powder
1 teaspoon Paprika
1/2 teaspoon salt
4 ounces tomato sauce

1/2 teaspoon ground black pepper
1/2 teaspoon cayenne pepper
2 cups water
1 clove garlic
1 teaspoon cumin
1 14-1/2 ounce can tomatoes, chopped

Add the venison and onion to the oil, cooking over medium heat until venison is brown. Add the remaining ingredients, cover, and simmer about on hour or until the meat is tender (this will vary with heat-long and slow is better). Stir occasionally while cooking. Correct seasonings to taste. Thicken with one tablespoon of flour mixed with two tablespoons of warm water.

Venison Chili

Chad Heeb, NY

1 pound ground venison
2 pounds venison sausage
1 onion
1 green pepper
2 fresh tomatoes
1 can tomato paste
2 cans whole tomatoes
1/2 cup hot chicken wing sauce

Chili powder
Salt
Pepper
Garlic
Italian seasoning
1 can dark kidney beans
1 can light kidney beans
1 can baked beans

Open tomato paste, and whole peeled tomato cans and put in crock pot on low. Dice up two fresh tomatoes, add a layer of chili powder, wing sauce, salt, pepper, garlic, and Italian seasoning. Cook ground venison in separate pan add that in crock pot. Cook venison sausage, cut and add to crock pot. Add the dark red kidney beans, light red kidney beans and baked beans. Chop up the onion and add another layer of pepper, wing sauce, chili powder, salt pepper, garlic, and Italian seasoning. Cook on low for 6 to 8 hours after first serving keep crock pot on keep warm.

Eli's Extreme Venison Chili

Eli Eccles, IN

2 pounds ground venison
2 cans hot chili beans
2 cans chopped green chiles
1 medium onion

1 can tomato juice
Salt and pepper
Chili powder

Brown venison. Chop the onion and mix it with the meat. Drain. Mix in the beans and the chiles. Stir well. Add the tomato juice, salt, pepper and chili powder to taste.

En Fuego Deer Chili

Leslie Hawkinson, NE

Shredded venison
8 cans tomato sauce
2 cans chili beans
1 onion

1 pint jar of habanero peppers, crushed
1 pint jar of jalapeño peppers, crushed
Bay leaves

Shred the venison by hand, don't grind it! Brown the shredded venison in a large cast iron skillet with unsalted butter and onion slices. Add both venison and onions to other ingredients and simmer for 6 to 8 hours. Serve with buttered biscuits and chocolate milk.

Venison Chili

Keith Corrigan, MI

4 tablespoons unsalted butter
1 red onion, chopped
4 cloves garlic, minced
4 tablespoons dark brown sugar
3 cups red wine
4 tablespoons red wine vinegar
4 tablespoons tomato paste
4 cups low-sodium chicken broth
1 teaspoon ground cumin

1/2 teaspoon cayenne pepper
1/2 teaspoon chili powder
2 tablespoons chopped fresh cilantro
4 tablespoons canola oil
10 slices cooked bacon, diced
2 pounds venison stew meat,
    trimmed and finely diced
2 cups black beans,
    cooked and drained

Melt the butter in a large pot over medium heat. Stir in the onion and garlic, and saute for 3 to 4 minutes. Stir in the brown sugar and saute for 2 to 3 more minutes. Then stir in the red wine, vinegar, tomato paste, chicken stock, cumin, cayenne pepper, chili powder, cilantro and salt. Simmer for 30 to 35 minutes, or until the mixture is reduced by about half. Meanwhile, heat the oil in a large skillet over medium-high heat. Stir in the bacon and fry for 3 to 4 minutes, or until the bacon is browned. Move the bacon to one side of the skillet and add the venison to the empty side of the skillet. Season the meat with salt to taste and saute the meat for 15 minutes, or until well browned. Stir in the beans and toss all together. Transfer this mixture to the simmering pot. Mix everything together thoroughly and let simmer for about 20 more minutes.

Black Bean Venison Chili

Roy Dancy, GA

3 tablespoons olive oil
1/2 pound bacon, chopped into small pieces
3 pounds of ground venison (no fat added)
4 cups chopped yellow onion
4 to 6 garlic cloves, minced
1/3 cup chili powder
3 tablespoons of ground cumin
1-1/2 tablespoons of dried oregano
1 teaspoon of cayenne pepper
6 cups of beef broth
1 cup of yellow cornmeal
Two 16-ounce cans of black beans
Dash of salt

Heat 1 tablespoon of oil in large skillet and add bacon pieces. Cook over medium heat until bacon is crisp and brown. Remove bacon from skillet and place on paper towel to drain. Leave drippings in pan. Place ground venison in skillet with drippings and cook uncovered until meat browns and all red disappears. Drain browned venison and place into a large pot along with the bacon. Heat remaining 2 tablespoons of olive oil in skillet and add chopped onions and garlic. Cook over low heat until tender and onions are translucent. Add cooked onions into pot with venison and bacon. Stir in salt, chili powder, oregano, cayenne pepper and cook over medium heat, stirring often about 5 minutes. Add in remaining ingredients except for cornmeal, stir together, lower heat and simmer for about 90 minutes. Add the cup of cornmeal and cook stirring often about 45 minutes over low heat. Sour cream can be added on top as an optional garnish when served.

Venison Chili

William Desnoyers, NY

1/2 cup peanut oil, plus 1/2 cup
3 pounds venison shoulder,
    cut into 3/4-inch cubes
1 green pepper, diced
2 cups diced red onion
3 celery stalks, diced
3 jalapeños, diced
4 cloves garlic, minced
1/4 cup chili powder
2 tablespoons dried Mexican oregano
2 tablespoons ground coriander
2 tablespoons ground cumin

2 tablespoons ground cayenne
2 tablespoons ground chipotle
1 teaspoon ground cinnamon
2 cups veal stock
1 bottle beer
1 small can chipotles, pureed
2 cups cooked black beans
One 16-ounce can,
    peeled and diced tomatoes
Grated manchego, for garnish
Chopped pickled jalapeño, for garnish

Add 1/2 cup of oil in a large saucepan and heat. Add the venison and brown, in batches, and set aside. Add pepper, onion, celery, jalapeño, and garlic and saute over a low heat until they are tender.

Add the remaining oil, all of the dry spices and the venison and stir, completely incorporating the ingredients. Add the stock, beer, beans, tomatoes, and chipotle puree.

Cover and simmer for 2 to 3 hours or until venison is fork tender. Check for seasoning and serve. Serve with grated manchego and pickled jalapeño.

Cowboy Chili

Paul Doty, NY

3 pounds venison,
    cut into 1/2 to 3/4-inch cube
1/4 cup pork lard or Crisco
4 tablespoons chili powder
3 dried red peppers, crushed

1 tablespoon dried oregano
1 teaspoon whole dried cumin, bruised
2 cloves garlic, sliced
2 teaspoon salt and black pepper to taste
3 onions, peeled and chopped at fireside

* These instructions are for making at fireside when camping out or on the trail. The spices should be combined at home and carried in a can or plastic bag, the lard and garlic should be packaged separately. You can make chili powder from scratch by mixing ground cayenne, oregano, cumin and salt in a 3:2:1:1 ratio. Use a dutch oven, 3-quart size or better, nestled in a generous bed of coals. It's easiest if the supply fire is a couple

feet away, giving you a chance to work over the pot, adding fresh coals to the cooking area as needed. Brown the meat in the lard, half at a time. With a large slotted spoon set the browned meat aside, adding more lard as necessary. After all the meat is well browned, pour off any extra grease. Combine the meat, chili powder and all the spices. Dice and add the garlic. Stir the meat vigorously, coating each piece with the spices, and continue cooking over lower heat for 10 to 12 minutes. It may be necessary to remove the kettle from the coals to prevent burning, but the heat of the pot should be sufficient to allow the herbs and peppers to soften and blend. Add enough water to cover the meat. Return to the fire with enough coals to bring the chili to a boil. Cover and simmer, stirring occasionally, for one hour. Grate or chop the onions finely and add to the chili. Continue cooking for an additional hour, adding more water as necessary until the onion dissolves.

Allow the chili to stand for 10 minutes before serving, skimming off any fat that rises to the top.

Venison Black Bean Chili

Colby Reynolds, OK

2 pounds venison roast, cut up
1 packet chili seasonings
2 teaspoons chili powder
1 teaspoon garlic powder
1 teaspoon cumin
1 large onion, chopped
Two 15-ounce cans black beans, drained
Two 14 1/2-ounce cans chili-style chopped tomatoes with juice
One 6-ounce can tomato paste
One 16-ounce refried beans with green chili
Salt and pepper, to taste
Sour cream
1 bunch green onions, sliced
1 cup shredded colby jack cheese

Cut the venison into 1-inch cubes. Turn the crock pot on low and add venison, chili seasoning, chili powder, garlic powder, and cumin. Add in chopped onion, beans, and 2 cans of chopped tomatoes. Cover and cook for 8 to 10 hours. Uncover and stir in tomato paste, refried beans and the salt and pepper. Serve at once, garnish with sour cream, green onions and cheese.

Rosenbaum Venison Chili

George Rosenbaum, CT

4 pounds ground venison with 1 pound pork fat trimmings (grind)
Spices: minced garlic, onion, fennel seed, chopped red pepper, salt and pepper.
    Mix and leave set overnight
2 cans of beans, one kidney, one black
1 can tomatoes
1 package False Alarm Chili kit
2 onions, chopped

    Braise the chopped onions in hot olive oil, cover bottom of crock pot.
Braise the venison-pork fat, spices mixture in hot olive oil. Place a layer of
meat on top of the onions. Mix in tomatoes and False Alarm chili kit. Turn on
crock pot. Cook for 3-4 hours. For the last hour, add the two cans of beans.

Texas Snakebite Chili

Bill Luell, TX

2 pounds ground venison
One 14½-ounce can of diced tomatoes or 1 cup fresh diced tomatoes
One 15-ounce can tomato sauce (thick and zesty kind the best)
1/2 cup chili pepper
1/2 tablespoon paprika
1/2 tablespoon comino (cumin)
1/2 tablespoon oregano, ground finely
1/2 tablespoon salt
1/2 tablespoon dried onion flakes or 1/4 cup finely chopped fresh onion
1/2 tablespoon garlic powder
2 teaspoons of red pepper (1/2 tablespoon if you want to fire it up!)
2 tablespoons of masa flour
1/4 cup warm water
One 15-ounce can of pinto beans (if desired)

    Brown venison, drain off fat. Add all ingredients except last three. Cook
for 30 minutes, stir occasionally. Stir masa and water together to make
thick, flowable mixture. Add to chili and stir. Add beans if desired. Simmer
another 30 minutes. While cooking, add more water or sauce as needed to
consistency desired.
    Serve with a sprinkle of Monterey jack cheese, a warm tortilla and a very
cold cerveza.

Damn Good Deer Chili

Sheri Williams, TX

Cooking spray
1 pound ground venison
1 cup chopped sweet onion
1 cup chopped green bell pepper
3 garlic cloves, minced
1 jalapeño pepper, seeded and chopped
2-1/2 tablespoons chili powder
1/2 teaspoon salt
1/2 teaspoon ground cumin
1/2 teaspoon black pepper
One 14 1/2-ounce can diced tomatoes, do not drain
One 14-ounce can chicken broth
1 can tomato paste
Optional:
One 15-ounce can red kidney beans, rinsed and drained
1/2 teaspoon ground red pepper

Coat pan with cooking spray. Add venison, and brown, stirring to crumble. Remove and drain, cover and keep warm. Spray pan again and cook the onion, bell pepper, garlic, and jalapeño until tender, stirring frequently. Stir in chili powder and next four ingredients. Add venison, diced tomatoes, chicken broth, and tomato paste, stirring until well combined; bring to a slow boil. Cover, reduce heat, and simmer 30 minutes. Optional: Add red kidney beans and red pepper, and cook, uncovered for an additional 15 minutes.

You Betcha Chili

Michael Mullins, MI

2 pounds ground venison
1 pound ground beef
2 or 3 medium jalapeños, chopped
1 large green pepper, chopped
1 medium onion, chopped
3 stalks celery, chopped
3 cans of small red kidney beans (a mix of dark and light if you prefer)
1 can tomato soup
1 large can stewed tomatoes, chopped

1 small can of tomato sauce
3 tablespoons chili powder
1 tablespoon red pepper powder
1 teaspoon curry
1/2 teaspoon cinnamon
1 rounded teaspoon cocoa powder
1 bottle of your favorite ale

In a large skillet, brown meat and drain. In a large crock pot combine all your tomato sauce and soup (no water), add all the chopped veggies and seasonings, drain and add beans (no need to rinse). Add the ground meat and stir well. Add salt and pepper to taste. Cook on low for 4 or 5. Enjoy the ale! For soupier chili you can add some tomato or V8 juice. We like to serve it over Fritos and top with grated cheddar.

Deer Chili

Charles Buzbee, FL

2 pounds venison
1 pound bacon
1 bell pepper
1 onion
Chili powder
Garlic

Cumin
Tabanero hot sauce
1 can diced tomatoes
2 cans tomato sauce
1 can tomato paste

Combine tomato sauce, tomato paste, chili powder, cumin, and diced tomatoes in a slow cooker. In a large skillet, fry the bacon to crispness, drain, and add to cooker. Add venison, bell pepper, onion and garlic to skillet, brown meat, stirring often. Add to cooker. Slow cook on high about 1 1/2 hours. Add hot sauce to taste.

Jim's Chili

Mark Arthur, OH

1 pound ground beef
1 pound ground venison
Chili seasoning
1 can mushroom pieces, drained
1 can diced tomatoes

1 can tomato sauce
1 can chili beans or kidney beans
1 teaspoon dehydrated onions
Garlic salt, salt and pepper to taste

Brown the beef and venison. I usually brown them separate and season the meat as it browns to lock in the flavor. In a pot, combine tomato sauce and 1 can water, tomatoes, mushrooms, dehydrated onions, garlic salt and chili seasoning. Simmer on low heat, stirring occasionally. Add the browned meats and continue to simmer, mix well. After simmering 15 to 20 minutes, add the beans and continue to simmer and stir for another 10 to 5 minutes. The trick to great chili is to slow cook it so the flavors blend well... just don't forget to stir it so it doesn't stick or burn. Serve and top with cheese (diced onions if desired), crackers, chips or corn bread.

Deer Chili Man

Neal Benson, IL

2 pounds ground venison
Two 16-ounce cans Bush's medium chili beans
2 packets Chili Man chili mix
One 16-ounce medium Old El Paso Thick n Chunky salsa
Two 10-ounce cans Rotel diced tomatoes and green chillies
One 14-1/2-ounce can diced tomatoes with garlic & onion
1 cup diced white onion
2 teaspoons of minced garlic

Mix all of the items except the deer meat in a crock pot and put on high for 1 hour. After mixing the items, brown the deer meat, and drain any fat away. Add the cooked venison to the crock pot. After 1 hour on high, put crock pot on low for at least 4 hours. The longer on low the better. Adding sour cream and shredded cheddar cheese can also turn this into a great dip for that football game party.

Chapter 10

Unconventional Venison

Oyster Venison

Tim Moquin, NH

1 venison backstraps quartered or 4 to 6 steaks
1/3 cup oyster sauce
1/3 cup honey
1/3 cup soy sauce
2 tablespoons ketchup
2 tablespoons sugar
2 to 3 cloves garlic, minced
1/4 teaspoon cinnamon
1/4 teaspoon curry
1/4 teaspoon ginger
1/4 teaspoon parsley

Set aside venison and combine all other ingredients in Zip-lock bag. Mix, then add venison. Marinate overnight. Grill to medium-rare. Leftover marinade can be heated and thickened on stove for sauce. Serve with wild grain rice and choice of vegetable.

Papa's Deer Neck Hash

Mary Baker, FL

3 to 5 pounds deer neck meat (untrimmed)
1/2 onion, finely diced
1 green bell pepper, finely diced
3 to 4 tablespoons butter
Salt, pepper, and garlic salt for seasoning
Sub rolls (or your favorite bread)
Shredded colby or monterey jack cheese
Chopped mushrooms (optional)

Put meat in slow cooker or roasting pan and season with salt and pepper and garlic salt generously. (Works best to leave overnight on low heat to ensure tenderness) Save a 1/2 cup of broth cooked out of meat for adding later. Melt butter in medium-large skillet; add onion and bell pepper and saute until tender. Chop neck meat with kitchen scissors or shears in about 1-inch pieces. Add meat to the skillet, and season as desired with more salt, pepper, and garlic salt. Brown the meat on medium-high heat for 5 to 8 minutes stirring occasionally, then add the broth back in and stir. Serve on a sub-roll or your favorite bread, add cheese and let melt. Makes a great Philly-Steak style sandwich, very moist! Also very good served as quesadillas, on a biscuit, or just by itself.

Corned Venison

Clay Whittaker, IN

2 cups water
6 tablespoons sugar-based curing mixture (such as Morton Tender Quick)
1/2 cup brown sugar
4 1/2 teaspoons pickling spice
1 tablespoon garlic powder
6 cups cold water
5 pounds boneless shoulder venison roast

Bring 2 cups of water to a boil in a saucepan over high heat. Stir in the curing mixture, brown sugar, pickling spice, and garlic powder; stir until dissolved then remove from the heat. Pour 6 cups of cold water into a 2-gallon container, and stir in the spice mixture. Place the boneless venison into the brine, cover and refrigerate.

Leave the venison in the refrigerator to brine for 5 days, turning the meat over every day.

To cook, rinse the meat well, place into a large pot, and cover with water. Bring to a boil, then reduce heat to medium-low, cover, and simmer for 4 hours. Remove the venison from the pot, and allow to rest for 30 minutes before slicing.

Jamaican Curry Venison

Michael Alleyne, FL   *Serves: 4*

1 pound of venison
1/4 cup oil
1 cups water
1 tomatoe, chopped
1 onion, chopped

2 tablespoons Jamaican Style curry powder
1/2 clove garlic, chopped
1 sprig thyme
2 slices hot pepper (optional)
Salt

Cut the Venison in 1 1/2-inch cubes. Brown (fry) curry powder, onions, garlic, tomatoes, thyme and pepper in oil. Add venison and brown rice (fry) for 5 minutes. Finally, add water, lower heat, cover and simmer for 30 to 45 minutes or until meat and rice is cook.

Best served with white rice.

Red Curry Venison Meatballs

Michael Childress, VA

Ground mild venison sausage
Red curry
Black pepper
Coconut milk

Olive oil
Beef stock
Basmati rice

Take 2 pounds of ground venison mild sausage, make into meatballs the size of ping-pong balls, brown in deep frying pan with olive oil. Add 1/2 cup of beef stock, teaspoon of black pepper then simmer for 20 minutes. Add 3 tablespoons of red curry powder, simmer 20 minutes. Add one can of coconut milk simmer 10 minutes, then add more red curry for desired taste. Serve over basmati rice, don't forget an ice cold beer for beverage.

Venison Cardiac Arrest

Bill Mayhew, MI

Venison heart
Apple (granny smith or Fuji preferred)
Onion
Green bell pepper
Red bell pepper

Morel mushrooms (lots!)
Ground red pepper
Salt
Olive oil

Clean and cube the heart, removing all valves and veins. Brown the heart in frying pan with Olive Oil, reduce to simmer. Dice up the apple and onion, add the onion to the heart. Slice up the bell peppers to bite- sized pieces. Add to Heart. Slice up the Morels, wash thoroughly. Add to the Heart. Add in the red pepper to taste (a few dashes should do).

Salt to taste. Cook Thoroughly. Serve alone or on a bed or rice or angel hair pasta. AWESOME! (In our camp, we have a rule: you MUST pack out the heart, unless destroyed, for supper that night. If you forgot to pack it out, you have to go back after it, after dark and get it.) This is a really different type recipe, but mouth watering. Guaranteed!

Breakfast Tacos

Vince Stigler, IN   *feeds four*

1 deer heart
4 green onions, chopped
1/2 red bell pepper, chopped
4 large farm fresh eggs, scrambled
2 tablespoons canola oil
1/2 teaspoon minced garlic
1/4 teaspoon cumin

1 cup cheddar cheese
1 package flour soft taco shells
Tabasco sauce or salsa
2 tablespoon Sirachi sauce
1 tablespoon Worcestershire sauce
Salt
Pepper

Trim one deer heart. Thin slice and marinade in Sirachi and Worcestershire sauce for 24 hours. Heat soft shells and cover. Heat oil in large iron skillet. Begin browning heart, onions, red peppers, When they begin to brown, add garlic and cumin. Cook until meat and veggies are nearly done, then add eggs, stirring into meat. Salt and pepper to taste.

Cook until eggs are almost completely solid, top eggs and meat with cheddar cheese and cover pan until cheese is melted, then plate. Fill you soft shell about 1/2 or 1/3 full, finish with salsa, Tabasco or both, enjoy!

Sweet and Sour Venison

Richard Kielpikowski, WI

1 8-ounce can pineapple chunks, in own juice
2 tablespoons corn oil
1 green pepper, cut in 1-inch squares
1 onion, cut in thin wedges
1 clove of garlic, minced

1 pound boneless venison, cut in thin strips
2 tablespoons cornstarch
1/2 cup light or dark corn syrup
1/4 cup cider vinegar
3 tablespoons soy sauce
2 tablespoons ketchup

Drain pineapple, reserve juice. In wok heat oil over medium heat. Add next 3 ingredients. Stir fry 2 minutes or until tender crisp, remove. Stir fry venison half at a time about 3 minutes, return venison to wok. In bowl stir together pineapple juice and remaining 5 ingredients, stir into wok. Add green pepper mix and pineapple. Bring to a boil over medium heat stirring constantly. Boil 1 minute, serve over rice.

Venison Crock Pot Touch of Japan

Shawn Pollard, NC

Several pounds of venison of your choice
1 bottle of Teriyaki sauce
3 tablespoons sesame oil
4 cloves garlic
1/4 brown sugar
1 can beef stock
Several tablespoons of Italian spices

1/2 teaspoon black pepper
I like mine spicy so I use a little red pepper (your taste)
1 tablespoon of Tony C's spice salt
1 onion chopped coarse
1 beer
1 cup of whiskey your choice

Take your venison and cube it up. 1-inch or better cubes works well.

First take 1/2 of the whiskey and make yourself a drink. Mix all other ingredients together.

Before you add the marinade to the meat taste and adjust to your liking. Some might want to add cinnamon or the like, other more adventurous fresh blackberries (blackberries and venison just seem to go together),. The longer you can do this I think the better.

Then put everything in the crock pot and cook as you would anything of the liking. Serve with rice bread, vegetables.

Oh yeah, and make sure you mix yourself another drink.

Venison Gyros

Jesus Armas Jr., FL

2 tablespoons olive oil
1 1/2 tablespoons ground cumin
1 tablespoon minced garlic
2 teaspoons dried marjoram
2 teaspoons ground dried rosemary
1 tablespoon dried oregano

1 tablespoon red wine vinegar
Salt and pepper to taste
3 pounds venison, cut into 1/4-inch thick strips
One 12-ounce package pita bread, warmed

Mix the olive oil, cumin, garlic, marjoram, oregano, rosemary, red wine vinegar, salt and pepper together in a large bowl. Add the venison, and toss to evenly coat. Cover the bowl with plastic wrap. Marinate the venison in the refrigerator at least 2 hours.

Heat a large skillet over medium-high heat. Cook the venison strips until the venison has browned on the outside and is no longer pink on the inside, about 8 minutes. Put the meat in warmed pitas to serve.

Joe's Venison Apple Sausage

Joe Majewski, IN

80 percent ground venison
20 to 30 percent pork
1 cup apple sauce
1 cup apple juice
1 tablespoon black pepper

4 tablespoons salt
2 tablespoons brown sugar
1 tablespoon sage
1/2 tablespoon cinnamon

Makes 10 pounds of sausage. Mix ingredients before stuffing in sausage casings. Tastes great on the grill.

Chapter 11
Elk & Moose

ELK

Elk Meat Burritos

Joseph Leslie Busch, OR

3 pounds elk meat
Soft tortillas
Refried beans
Shredded cheddar cheese

Sour cream
Chopped onion
Jalapeño sauce

Cook elk meat until it is completely done, heat up tortillas, heat refried beans until hot. Chop up some onions and saute them until they are soft, place elk meat on a soft tortilla add some refried beans sauted onion cheese and sour cream fold the ends over then the sides then add more cheese on top with more sauted onion and add a dash of jalapeño sauce, then enjoy (I can see your mouth watering all ready).

Elk Chili

Charlie Marvich, ID

2 pounds ground venison
1/4 cup vegetable oil
1 large onion, thinly sliced
2 cloves garlic, minced
1 large green pepper, cut into strips
3 tablespoons chili powder

2 teaspoons sugar
3 1/2 cups canned tomatoes
1 cup tomato sauce
1 cup water
1/2 teaspoon salt
2 cups pinto beans, cooked

Brown ground venison in oil, add onion, garlic and green pepper. Cook 5 minutes,stirring constantly. Add chili powder, sugar, tomatoes, tomato sauce, water and salt. Simmer 1 1/2 hours. If a thicker chili is desired, stir in 1 tablespoon flour mixed with 2 tablespoons of water. Just before serving add 2 cups cooked pinto beans.

Elk in Raspberry Marinade

Marinade
2 cups raspberries, smashed
1/3 cup chopped onion
1 teaspoon pepper flakes
(more or less depending on
how hot you wish)

1 to 2 cloves minced, garlic
1/4 cup fresh cilantro
3 tablespoons lime juice
1/4 cup port wine

Mix all ingredients and place in a bowl with a tight lid.

Best Elk

Doug Thalacker, IN

2 pounds venison (or other wild game)
cut into 1/2-inch wide strips
2 tablespoons butter

2 tablespoons olive oil
Salt and pepper to taste

Put sliced venison in the raspberry marinade and let it sit for 8 hours or over night. Shake the container a couple times to make sure that the meat is thoroughly covered.

Heat butter and oil on medium high skillet. Remove venison from marinade and sear both sides in the skillet. Cook until pink in center. Remove from skillet. And let sit on warmed plate covered with aluminum foil. Reduce the heat, add the marinade. Cook until the marinade is reduced to about half, 10 minutes.

Put venison on serving platter and pour raspberries over meat. Enjoy.

Barbecued Elk Burgers

Jared Brunen, MB

1 pound elk burger
1 onion
2 tablespoons oil
1/4 cup ketchup
1 cup chunk tomato, or tomato juice

1 cup water
1 teaspoon chili powder
Salt, pepper, and mustard (to taste)
1 tablespoon minute tapioca

Brown meat and onion in oil. In a separate bowl, combine ketchup, tomato, water, chili powder, salt, pepper, mustard, and minute tapioca. Add meat and simmer for 2 hours.

Italian Elk

Karl Berger, IL

1 boneless elk or venison chuck eye roast, about 3-1/2 pounds
Kosher salt and fresh ground pepper
1 medium onion, roughly chopped
1 tablespoon dried Italian seasoning (I make my own) see attached recipe below
2 teaspoosn crushed red pepper
6 cloves of fresh garlic, roughly chopped
1/2 cup of good red wine
4 cups of beef stock
3 to 4 sprigs of fresh thyme
2 tablespoons of vegetable oil
4 to 6 sub or hoagie rolls

Dried Italian seasoning recipe:
2 tablespoons dried basil
2 tablespoons dried oregano
2 tablespoons dried rosemary
2 tablespoons dried marjoram
2 tablespoons thyme

Mix all together and store in zip-lock bag. Preheat oven to 300° F and position rack in middle of oven. Sprinkle the roast liberally with salt and pepper on all sides. Heat the oil in a Dutch oven over medium-high heat. Brown the roast on all side until golden and caramelized (reduce the heat if the fat begins to smoke) once browned on all side remove from heat on set aside. Reduce heat to medium add onions to dutch oven and saute onions,stirring occasionally until just beginning to brown (8 to 10 minutes). Add the Italian seasoning and crushed red pepper and saute till fragrant, (30 seconds). Add garlic and saute till fragrant (30 seconds). Deglaze with red wine and cook until alcohol smell is diminished. Add beef stock and fresh thyme and bring to simmer.

Place the roast back into the pot with accumulated juices and place in the oven cover. Increase oven temp to 325°. Cook roast ,turning every 45 minuets, until very tender (falling apart), about 3 1/2 to 4 hours. Remove roast from pan when cool enough and place on a cutting board and let cool (until you can handle roast with your hands). Pour Jus (stock) from pan thru a fine mesh colander or cheese cloth and collect Jus. Place Jus pack in pot and place on stove top on low. Remove any fat from meat and shred meat with hands and place back into Jus pot. Serve on sub or hoagie rolls. (Don't forget to dump the rolls into the Jus!!!)

BBQ Elk Stew

Billy Nunes, OR

2 to 3 pounds of deer or
    elk rump roast
1 large walla walla sweet onion
3 large potatoes

1 clove of garlic
1 pint of Long Horn BBQ sauce
1 to 2 cups of water

Cut roast into 1-inch chunks. Cut onion and potatoes in 1-inch chunks. Crush garlic and dice finely. Put all ingredients into a crock-pot or large pot, add Long Horn BBQ sauce and 1 cup of water mix well and simmer on low. Add additional water to thin sauce to desired thickness.

Bachelor Dip

Kevin Coahran, IN

2 pounds elk meat
1 large jar of salsa con queso

2 tablespoons sour cream

Brown meat drain off grease, heat up large jar of salsa con queso. Blend meat and salsa con queso together in large bowl, stir in sour cream serve with big scoops corn chips.

Elk Rump N' Saddle with Baked Beans

Fritter and Waste the Hours in an off hand way.

First, Only the finest Elk be chosen for a feast such as this. None of the animal shall go to waste, so we make sure to pack away what we don't use in the freezer, after making it into either steaks or sausage. The bones can be used for a great Pho noodle soup in the winter, or for broth. We use the furs for blankets, and jackets. — Danica Enfantino, CA

Elk Rump N' Saddle
4 to 5 pounds elk premium meat, the finest cuts. The rest can be frozen (cutlets, ribs, tougher meat, the little bits ground to sausage)

Rub:
2 cups flour
2 tablespoons paprika
1 teaspoon cumin
Salt - depending on your family, we use about
    3 tablespoons - add a little at a time to make sure
    you don't overdo it
2 tablespoons sugar
1/4 cup Balsamic vinegar
Pinch of thyme
2 to 3 teaspoons fresh ground pepper
    (more depending on you)
2 tablespoons apple juice
Luke-warm water (enough to make it a bit moist)

Mix the Rub ingredients together in a bowl. Roll cuts in rub and set aside. I refrigerate them a bit, then roll them around again.

Time to get out the smoker, barbecue or oven...whichever you prefer. Set the heat to about 200° F and just barely get them cooking. You don't want them to cook yet.

Sauce/Marinade:
1 onion, chopped
1/2 cup or so olive oil
1 to 2 garlic, minced
1 to 2 cups broth: either beef stock or use the bones to make your own
    elk broth (to taste)
Salt and pepper, for flavor, about a spoonful each
Garlic salt, a dash
Onion powder, a dash
Seasoned salt, a dash
Thyme, only a sprinkle

In a large stew pot simmer over low-medium heat the onion, olive oil and garlic. Then add the rest of the marinade ingredients.

Add the rest of flour mixture from before, simmer until thick dip those suckers in once its cooled, and let em set in there for about 3 hours or so.

Once done marinating, set them out. The aroma will about set you off into southern bliss.

Now cook them how you like them. Me? I like mine bleeding.

Baked Beans
Any beans that tickle your fancy - use enough for your company
Water - enough to cook em plus a little for sauce
2 cups sugar
1/4 cup apple juice. I like to substitute a little of the sugar for the juice, all of it can
    be too sweet but the apple juice adds a heavenly aroma
2 tomatoes, chopped
Broth from either the elk or beef broth
Cream, just a dash
Salt and pepper
1 tablespoon onion powder
Paprika, a dash for spice
Use the marinade from earlier

Should have a pretty thick sizzlin' bean heap. Put some cilantro and a touch of lemon in, then either cook up some wild rice, or some roasted barbecued vegetables and you've got yourself a meal!!

Elk Meat Burritos

Joseph Leslie Busch, OR

3 pounds elk meat
Soft tortillas
Refried beans
Shredded cheddar cheese

Sour cream
Chopped onion
Jalapeño sauce

Cook elk meat until it is completely done heat up tortillas heat refried beans until hot. Chop up some onions and saute them until they are soft place elk meat on a soft tortilla add some refried beans sauted onion cheese and sour cream fold the ends over then the sides then add more cheese on top with more sauted onion and add a dash of jalapeno sauce, then enjoy (I can see your mouth watering all ready).

MOOSE

Moose Roast

Al Broecker, WI

2 to 4 pounds venison, moose,
   elk, roast
Slow cooker
Water or wine
1/2 to 1 package dry onion soup mix

Vegetables (potato, carrot, onion...
   your choice)
1 cup water (wine if you like,
   or other booze)

In a slow cooker on medium heat, place the meat, add water, or wine, the dry onion soup mix, cook for 3 to 4 hours, then add vegetables. Cook for another 3 to 4 hours or until vegetables are done. Take out slice meat and make some gravy out of the liquids.

If you have friends who don't like wild meat, try this on them. They will not know what they are eating. ENJOY!!!!!

Sweet Bacon-Wrapped Moose Tenderloin

Jared Brunen, MB

2 pounds venison tenderloin (deer, elk, or moose)	3 cups brown sugar
1/2 pound bacon (thin sliced)	2 cups regular soy sauce
	1/4 cup white sugar

Mix brown sugar and soy sauce together in a bowl. They should combine nicely into a soupy soy liquid. Put deer loin in a cooking tray and pour brown sugar/soy sauce mixture over loin. Roll tenderloin over in mixture, completely covering it. Let meat marinate in mixture at least 3 hours or overnight in fridge. It's best to marinate for 8 hours if you have the time. Also GREAT to use a Food Saver or other vacuum device to vacuum pack/seal the meat with marinade. With this method, you can achieve overnight-level marinade in just a couple hours!

Remove loin from tray, and place on a slotted bake sheet with a drip pan or aluminum foil below to catch dripping. Don't throw away marinade. Wrap a piece of bacon around the very end of the tenderloin, securing the bacon strip with a toothpick. Repeat this process until the entire loin is wrapped in 10 or so bacon "loops." The tenderloin should look like an arm with a bunch of wrist watches on it, the watches being the bacon strips.

Drizzle remaining marinade over deer loin. You can continue to baste the loin with the marinade throughout the cooking process with either a brush or a turkey baster. Place on center rack in oven and bake at 350° F for 30 to 40 minutes. This should cook the meat to about medium. For those of you who prefer rare meat (like me), cut the time to 25 to 30 minutes and then follow with the OPTION 2 step below regarding searing.

OPTION 1 - with about 10 minutes of cooking time left, you can lightly dust the top of the loin with white sugar. This creates a sweet crust on top of the bacon. Might be too sweet for some. Try doing it on just HALF of the loin to see if you like it!

OPTION 2 - For a crispier crust and crispier bacon, remove Loin from oven and place the Loin(s) directly on a Grill over medium-high heat to sear the bacon and outer loin. (Thanks to all of you reviewers who taught me this. It›s a great step for those of us who like a cooked crust and a pink center).

Remove from oven and place on cutting board. Using a knife, cut the loin between each strip of bacon so that you have many pieces of meat, each with their own toothpick. You can eat these pieces directly from the toothpick or remove the toothpick and eat like steak. You can thank me later. The next day, try the leftovers on a wheat bun with spicy barbecue sauce for an awesome leftover sandwich.

Oregano Moose Steak

Duncan Horner, BC

2 tablespoons olive or vegetable oil
1 tablespoon oregano

1 teaspoon coarse salt
Fresh cracked black pepper (to taste)

In a bowl add the olive oil, oregano, coarse salt and pepper. Mix it up and it should have quite a thick consistency. Spread it on your deer chops or moose steak and leave it to marinate for a little while in the fridge. Then just grill your meat however you like it. The beauty of this recipe is how simple it is. As there are only four ingredients it is easy to adjust the quantities until you get your perfect flavour. This is pretty much how we cook every deer chop or moose steak we eat in our house. Delicious!

4-Alarm Moose Chili

Fred Veltman, NY

2 pounds moose stew meat
2 tablespoons olive oil
2 cloves garlic
10 husked and chopped tomatillos
1 green pepper, chopped
1 onion, chopped

4 to 6 jalapeño peppers,
    seeded and diced
1 tablespoon paprika
1 14.5-ounce can stewed tomatoes
1 12-ounce can beef broth
3 tablespoon chopped fresh cilantro

1. In a Dutch oven, brown cubed venison in hot oil.
2. Add remaining ingredients and bring to a boil.
3. Simmer two hours or until meat is tender.

Chapter 12

Turkey

Wild Turkey Breast Steaks

Tim Gebers, NE

Wild turkey breast
Italian dressing

Trim all fat from turkey breast cut 1-inch wide steaks (across the grain) of the breast.

In a lidded plastic container place 'steaks', cover with Italian dressing let marinate for 24 hours, couple of times during the 24 hours give the container a shake just to make sure marinade is getting to all sides of the meat, discard dressing after marinating.

Grill on medium-high heat turning frequently to avoid burning (because of the dressing) cook to 160° F to 165°, can brush on more dressing last few minutes of grilling or use any barbecue sauce, if cooked correctly you'll swear you are eating a lean pork chop.

Chris Barton's Wild Turkey Breast

Chris Barton, KY

Wild turkey breast
Turkey gravy
Poultry seasoning
Onions
Carrots

Celery
Salt
Pepper
Stuffing mix

Place turkey breast in crock-pot on high for about 4 hours along with seasonings and gravy. After 3 hours place vegetables in with meat. Prepare stuffing mix separate. Finish the turkey by placing on top of stuffing and adding gravy on top and vegetables on side.

Wild Turkey Country Style

Dave Burgess, TN

2 turkey breasts
Egg
Flour
Salt and pepper

Buttermilk
Butter
Cooking oil

Filet the turkey breasts and soak over night in buttermilk. Slice very thin and pound to tenderize. Dredge in egg batter and coat in the flour. Salt and pepper to taste. Fry in a lightly oiled pan until done on both sides prepare country gravy with the drippings in the pan with water ,flour and salt and pepper. Serve with mashed potatoes and fresh green beans. You'll love it!

Wild Turkey Cream of Mushroom/Wild Rice Soup

Douglas Pickle, VA

1/2 wild turkey breast or other part of the turkey
4 to 6 carrots and celery, cut into slices
Half of a large sweet onion
Two to three 32-ounce cans chicken broth
One 10-ounce can cream of chicken soup
Two to three boxes of Rice-a-Roni long grain/wild rice and seasons that is in the box
One large can of mushrooms
1/2 to 1 cup of whipping cream
McCormick's Grill Mates Montreal chicken seasoning
Dry sherry
Hot sauce of your choice

Cut the turkey up into small pieces and cook in frying pan...use olive oil and season the turkey with McCormick's Grill Mates Montreal chicken seasons, black pepper, garlic salt and a little dry sherry. Add the turkey with all the juices from the frying pan into the pot when its time...see below...

Take a large pot and add olive oil and cook the carrots, celery, and onions until tender. Add the chicken broth, rice, hot sauce to your taste and mushrooms cook for 30 to 45 minutes, bring to a boil and then turn down to simmer. Stir regular so not to burn on the bottom of the pot. After cooking for 45 minutes, add the whipping cream and wild turkey and cook for another 15 to 30 minutes.

Award-Winning Turkey Chili

Bill Luell, TX

1 pound ground turkey
2 onions, diced
1 green pepper, diced
1 tablespoon jalapeño, finely chopped
One 14-ounce can Mexican-style
    tomatoes (like Rotel)
Two 8-ounce cans tomato sauce
2 tablespoons cumin
2 tablespoons chili powder

1 teaspoon salt
1/2 teaspoon cayenne pepper
1/2 teaspoon paprika
    (smoked if you can find it)
One 14-ounce can kidney beans,
    drained and rinsed
One 14-ounce can black beans,
    drained and rinsed
1 cup water

Toppings:
Sour cream
Cheddar cheese
Green onion

Cook ground meat with onions and peppers in Dutch oven. Drain excess grease and add tomatoes, seasonings, and water, bring to a boil. Add beans, cover and simmer 1 to 2 hours. Serve with toppings.

WPTC Venison, Wild Turkey and Shrimp Fajitas

Adam Polvi, GA

1 venison backstrap, cut up into thin strips
2 wild turkey breasts, cut into thin strips
1/2 pound of peeled, no-tail raw shrimp
3 bell peppers (green, red and/or yellow), cut into long strips
2 medium onions, cut not chopped
Fajita seasoning
2 packages of large flour tortillas
Mexican shredded cheese
Salsa
One 16-ounce sour cream
Small bottle of Italian dressing

Marinate venison in the Italian dressing for a hour. Not too much dressing, just enough to coat the meat.

Mix the turkey in with the venison along with a pack of fajita seasoning. Mix well. Coat the bottom of a large skillet with olive oil. Bring to medium heat. Toss the deer and turkey in and simmer till almost done. Then throw in the shrimp, peppers, and onions. Stir fry till pepper and onions are soft and the shrimp is pink. I also like have yellow rice with this meal so get ya some of that as well. Directions are easy.

Fill the tortilla up with the fajitas, cheese, salsa, sour cream and roll the bad boy up and get to eat'n! Don't forget the rice.

Parmesan-Encrusted Wild Turkey Fingers

Martha Denka, SC

1 wild turkey breast
1 quart peanut oil
I bottle your favorite ranch dressing
1 container of parmesan cheese

Remove all silver skin and connecting tissue from the turkey breast and cut into thin strips. Thoroughly mix the ranch dressing and Parmesan cheese in a deep bowl. Drag each strip through this mixture and then drop into the peanut oil that was preheated to 400° F in a deep frying pan. The fingers are ready when they achieve an even golden brown color.

BLT with Avocado and Turkey

William Keys, WY

Bacon
Lettuce
Tomato

Avocado
Turkey

Stake all ingredients on top of toasted bread smothered with mayo.

Turkey Noodle Soup

Duane Hawkins, MO

1 quart turkey stock
1 rib celery, finely chopped
1 large carrot, finely chopped
1/4 cup onion, finely chopped

1 cup chopped leftover wild turkey
1/4 pound thin spaghetti noodles, broken
Salt and pepper to taste

Broth to a boil, add vegetables and cook until vegetables are tender about 8 minutes. Add turkey and noodles, cook until pasta is al dente. Add salt and pepper to taste.

Turkey Pot Pie

Ken Hockensmith, OH

2 to 3 cups cubed turkey
One 16-ounce jar of pre-made beef gravy (I prefer to boil a couple cups of broth
    and 1/2 cup flour and some milk to make a gravy)
One 16-ounce bag frozen peas and carrots, diced
2 to 3 small potatoes, diced
1 tablespoon celery salt or to taste
1 tablespoon pepper or to taste
Two 9-inch pie crusts
2 onions
2 quarts water
2 egg whites, optional

Combine venison, onions, salt, pepper and water in pressure cooker
cook on high 30 minutes, drain after cooling combine all ingredients and
mix all except onions pour into pie shell cover with second crust, cuts
several vent slits in top crust cook 350° F for 1 hour, egg whites on top crust
give a golden brown color.

Pie crust can be made from scratch or pre-made (use Lard if making from
scratch) grease and flour pan with bottom crust,

Wild Turkey Feet Stew

Carl Kozak, WI

2 pounds turkey feet (one set of turkey feet weighs about 1/2 pound)
5 potatoes, cut in eighths
4 onions, quartered
1 cup green beans
1 clove garlic, minced
Salt and pepper

Cut nails and wash feet. Place in stockpot. Cover with water. Add
potatoes, onions, carrots, green beans, bay leaf, garlic, salt and pepper
to season. Simmer until tender. Remove bay leaf before serving. 6 to 8
servings.

Chapter 13

Game Birds

Sherried Duck

William McCorquodale, NC   *Serves 4*

2 tablespoons olive oil
2 tablespoons butter
4 ducks, halved lengthwise
3 tablespoons flour
2 cups chicken broth
1/2 cup of sherry
Salt and pepper to taste

Heat olive oil and butter in a heavy skillet; cook ducks until browned.
Place ducks in a 2 1/2 quart casserole, add flour to pan drippings and
lightly brown. Stir in broth and sherry. Season to taste. Pour over ducks,
cover and bake at 350° F for 1 hour or until tender. Wild rice compliments
the duck.

Wild Drunk Duck

Gary Hickingbottom, LA

1 or 2 wild ducks (mallards)
One 16-ounce can of favorite beer
3 tablespoons of Tony's seasoning or favorite wild game seasoning
2 onions, quartered
4 potatoes, quartered
2 cups of water
3 liter plastic bottle

Cut top of bottle to bottom of neck, place ducks, seasoning, beer, and water in bottle, place in fridge for 2 hours. Preheat oven on 350° F , place potatoes and onions in casserole dish. Place ducks and 1/2 cup of liquid in and cover. Cook for 1 1/2 hours or till fork tender. ENJOY!

Candied Duck

Jeremy Johnson, MN

2 pounds of cubed duck
1/2 cup of flour
1/2 cup of brown sugar
2 peeled and cored apples
1 medium onion
Salt
Pepper
Lawry's seasoning salt
Cooking oil

Slice apples and onion 1/4 thick place flat on cookie sheet, sprinkle with brown sugar, let stand will you brown game.

Roll game in flour, fry in 1/4 of oil 375° F for 2 minutes per side, season with salt, pepper, and Lawry's.

When all game is browned place in crock-pot, add apple and onion and all juices accumulated on cookie sheet, cook for 4 hours on high, then turn to low and serve when ready to eat.

Pheasant Tacos

John Bush, CO

1 1/2 pounds pheasant meat
4 cups water
1 teaspoon salt
1/3 teaspoon pepper
1/2 teaspoon garlic powder

1 teaspoon onion powder
2 teaspoon chili powder
1 teaspoon dry oregano
1/4 teaspoon cumin

Add all of the ingredients in a medium to large sauce pan and bring it to a boil and boil for about 10 minutes. Reduce heat to low to medium-low and simmer for about 30 minutes with the lid cracked. You're looking for a nice little bubble.

After about 40 minutes drain most of the water leaving a small amount in the meat. Go ahead and shred the meat with using 2 forks. Meat is ready to make your tacos.

Braised Bacon-Wrapped Blue Cheese Goose Breast

Paul Krupa, NY

4 goose breast halves or more if you're hungry and feeding a few friends
1 cup crumbled blue cheese (substitute gorgonzola if you prefer)
Bacon, thick sliced
1 cup red wine, your choice, I prefer Chianti - drink the rest while preparing and
    cooking to pass the time
1/4 cup lemon juice
1/2 cup olive oil
1 tablespoon honey
Couple sprigs each of rosemary, thyme and parsley
1 to 2 bay leaves
3-4 cloves garlic, crushed or minced, or however much you like
Salt, dash into marinade
Hot pepper, minced - like a cubano, jalapeño, habanero or crushed red pepper

Breast geese removing all shot and all fat.

Mix wine, lemon juice olive oil, honey, spices in a gallon sealable bag. Place goose breast halves in bag mix thoroughly to coat, seal and marinate for 8 hours or overnight. Remove breasts, pat dry, discard marinade. Slice open goose breasts without cutting all the way through to make a pocket for the blue cheese. Wrap each stuffed goose breast with a slice of thick cut bacon and hold in place with tooth picks. Making sure each breast is covered with bacon

Pre-heat oven to 350° F. In a medium-hot to hot cast iron pan or Dutch oven, sear goose breasts on all sides. Remove from heat, add some wine to the bottom of the pan, just enough to wet the bottom, cover and place pan in pre-heated oven and continue cooking for 30 minutes until med to medium-rare. I like mine medium-rare.

Remove and let them set for 10 minutes. Then slice across the grain and plate on a bed of spring green salad or fresh baby spinach or if you prefer, garlic mashed potatoes.

Home Brew Grouse Stew

Matthew Huntley, NB

1 to 2 cans of your friends beer
2 pounds or so of grouse meat chunks
Carrots
Potatoes
Turnip
Celery
Onion
Green pepper
Garlic clove
Can of mushrooms
Any spices that smell good
   in the cupboard
Soy sauce
Worcestershire sauce

Pour 1 can of beer in a large frying pan, throw the chunked grouse meat in, add spices to the pan from the cupboard, I like chili powder, celery salt, steak spice, pepper, a bit of mild hot sauce. Add worcestershire sauce, soy sauce until the beer turns brown or light brown. Heat this on medium heat until meat is darkened or almost cooked. Add the other beer if you haven't drank it and turn heat off. Dice up vegetables, garlic clove into large pot or slow cooker. Add the frying pan full of meat as well as the liquid in the pan. Cook on low heat for 6 to 10 hours on low heat. Serve after a long day in the woods. Enjoy.

Dove Poppers

Shane Andersen, NE

A couple dozen freshly dressed dove breasts
2 dozen large jalapeños
2 pound bacon
1 pound box cream cheese
1 box toothpicks

Cut stems out of top of jalapeños without slicing them all the way open remove seeds. Add cream cheese into jalapeños. Cook bacon slightly to remove rawness. Take jalapeño and dove breast and wrap with bacon, using a couple of toothpicks skewer the jalapeño and dove with bacon wrap till they are solid and wont fall apart on grill. Then throw 'em all on the grill, cook till cream cheese begins to seep out of jalapeños or until bacon is slightly crisp. Not to crisp cause the dove breast doesn't take more than 4 minutes to cook over hot coals on charcoal or medium high heat of a gas grill. Nothing but a plate and fingers needed after that, enjoy.

Country-Fried Dove

Timothy Briggs, OH

Dove breasts
Cornmeal

Pepper
Lemon juice

Mix pepper and lemon juice, dip breasts in. Then roll in cornmeal then fry until golden brown.

Partridge Surprise

Mitch Krug, WI

4 partridge breasts
4 large potatoes, peeled and cubed
2 stalks celery
4 large carrots, peeled
6 strips bacon

1 large onion
1/2 stick butter
2 cans cream of mushroom soup
2 small cans mushrooms

Cube partridge breasts and saute in butter. Preheat oven to 350° F. Boil potatoes, celery, and carrots (chop them up so it goes quicker). Slice bacon into small bits and fry. After they are done, put to the side. Take potatoes, celery, and carrots and place in a casserole dish. Dump the cream of mushroom soup over the top. Add a little water so the veggies don't burn to the bottom. Layer the partridge on top of the soup mix. Place the mushrooms and bacon on top of the partridge. Slice the onion and place the slices randomly over the top. Cut the butter into small chunks and place on top of the onions. Salt and pepper to taste. Cover the casserole dish and place in oven at 350° for 45 minutes. Be prepared for your guests to rave over such a fine meal.

Best Dove Recipe

Matthew Smith, PA

Boneless dove breasts, cut in 2
Your favorite seasonings
Large jalapeño peppers
Cream cheese
Onion slices

Green pepper, cut into strips
Maple flavored bacon
Favorite BBQ sauce
Toothpicks

Season the dove to taste with your favorite seasonings. Remove the tips and stems from the jalapeños. Slice lengthwise in half and remove the seeds. Spread some cream cheese into each pepper half. Insert one piece of dove into the pepper. Top with a slice of onion and green pepper. Wrap with a slice of bacon and secure with toothpicks. Repeat with the rest of the ingredients. Grill over medium heat. When the bacon is done, doves are done. Baste with barbecue sauce when just about done.

Serve and enjoy.

Roast Duck

Rodney Kehrer, IL

4 whole ducks
1 cup flour
3 tablespoons kosher salt
3 tablespoons cracked pepper
3 tablespoons rosemary, plus extra

1 cup vegetable oil
1 large onion, sliced
1 bunch celery, chopped
2 cups chicken broth
4 cloves garlic

Preheat oven to 350° F. Combine flour, salt, pepper and rosemary to create coating mix. Roll duck in the coating mix, covering completely. Heat vegetable oil in a skillet. Brown duck on all sides, remove and set aside. Saute onion and celery in the same skillet and oil. Pour onion, celery, and all dripping in roasting pan. Add duck breast up. Add chicken broth. Cover pan with aluminum foil and roast for 1 hour in oven. With 10 minutes left, crush a clove of garlic on each duck, sprinkle with extra rosemary, and replace foil. Serve on bed of wild rice with a side salad of spring greens garnished with mandarin oranges.

Tea-Smoked Grouse

Nina Rose Dwyer, AK

A few good-sized grouse
1 tablespoon peppercorn
1 teaspoon five spice powder
2 tablespoons coarse salt
3 tablespoons Chinese black tea
2 teaspoons brown sugar
1/4 cup white rice (uncooked)

2 teaspoons sesame oil
2 tablespoons soy sauce
1/2 teaspoon ground ginger
1/4 cup dry sherry
2 teaspoons lime juice
Splash of Asian Chili sauce

Toast peppercorn in a dry skillet then grind with mortar/ pestle with the salt and five spice powder. Rub generously over grouse and cover with plastic wrap and refrigerate overnight.

Line the bottom of a wok with heavy foil. Mix the rice, tea and brown sugar and mound on the foil. Place a bamboo steamer on top and space grouse evenly on racks. Cover and cook over high heat and hot smoke for 12 minutes. Until smoky brown and cooked fully.

While grouse are smoking, add ginger, soy sauce, wine and sesame oil to a saucepan and bring to a boil. Brush on grouse right before serving. ENJOY! :)

Golden Quail

Joe Sinclair, MD

6 quail breast, split
1 teaspoon salt
1 tablespoon black pepper
3 cups sifted flour

1 tablespoon lemon juice
2 cups whole milk
1 stick of butter (not vegetable oil)

Wash breast and let drain. Put breast in bowl, add lemon juice and stick in fridge for 1 to 2 hours to marinate. Mix flour, salt, and pepper into a bowl. When ready to cook heat frying pan on medium heat while preparing breast. Place 1/2 stick of butter in pan and let melt. Place breast into milk in a bowl, shake off excessive milk and place into flour,salt and pepper coating, completely covering breast. Add breast to warm frying pan cooking for 4 to 5 minutes before turning over. After turning, add the other half stick of butter. Turning until desired brownness. Do not over cook or cook too fast. Serve warm. This will feed 2 to 3 people.

Chapter 14

Other Game

Wild Game Stew

Dennis McClure, MI

2 quarts venison broth
2 wild rabbits
1 squirrel
1 pound venison stew meat
4 or 5 potatoes, diced medium
1 to 2 garlic cloves, chopped

3 to 4 carrots
2 teaspoons onion powder
1 tablespoon garlic powder
Salt and pepper to taste
1 cup diced onion

Boil the bones of a deer for 45 minutes [after you butcher it] and remove the bones. In venison broth add 2 wild rabbits and 1 squirrel. Add onion powder, garlic powder, and salt and pepper. Bring to a boil and cook at a slow boil, cook until the meat falls off the bones, remove the bones after cooking about 3 to 4 hours.

Add venison stew meat and carrots, cook for 1 hour. Then add potatoes, onions, and garlic cloves. Cook on low heat until done. Mix flour and water to make gravy and add to the pot, simmer until thick.

Rabbit Chop Suey

Robert Szychulski, MI

1 rabbit
1 medium size bag of baby carrots
1 can of Campbell's cream of celery soup. Plus one can of water
1 can of Campbell's golden mushroom soup
1 can of mushroom gravy

Boil rabbit until the meat falls off the bone. Slice baby carrots in half. Mix rabbit meat, carrots, and rest of ingredients in crock-pot for about 3 hours on high. Prepare pot of white rice. Serve over rice. Also can be made with deer meat by boiling meat and remove scum for top of water. Cut deer meat in small pieces and mix in crock-pot with about ingredients. Will make 6 to 7 heaping dishes. It is delicious.

South Dakota Jambalaya

Jason Houser, IL

1 pound venison back strap
6 to 8 quail
10 ounces rabbit
4 1/2 cups chicken stock
1/2 cup dry white wine
1 teaspoon saffron
3/4 cup plus 2 tablespoons olive oil
1/2 cup green bell pepper, diced
10 cloves garlic, minced
2 cups scallions, chopped

1 1/2 cups pearl onions
3 ripe tomatoes, crushed and drained
1/2 cup frozen lima beans
2 cups canned artichoke hearts,
    quartered
1/2 cup peas
3 teaspoons sweet paprika
4 sprigs rosemary
3 cups short-grained rice
Salt and pepper, to taste

Season the meats with salt and pepper and grill to medium-rare. When the meats are cool enough to handle, cut into 1/2-inch pieces and set aside. Bring the stock, wine and saffron to a low simmer in a medium saucepan. Heat the olive oil in a large, deep cast-iron skillet over high heat until almost smoking, then add the green pepper, garlic, scallions and onions. Cook for about 5 minutes or until softened. Reduce the heat to medium-high and add the tomatoes, lima beans, artichoke hearts, peas, paprika and rosemary. Cook for another 2 minutes. Stir the rice into the pan until it is well coated with oil. Add the warm wine mixture to the pan, and simmer, stirring until no longer soupy but still very moist. Add the meats to the pan and remove it from the heat. Cover with a lid or foil. Let sit for another 10 to 15 minutes. Salt and pepper to taste. Serve.

Bear Burgers

James Bloxom, VA

5 pounds bear burger, no fat added
1-ounce McCormick Grill Mates hamburger or Grill Mates Spicy Montreal Steak
    seasoning
2 tablespoons granulated garlic
3/4 cup onions, chopped
1 pound mild cheddar cheese, shredded

Cook on smoker grill or offset cook on regular charcoal grill for about 1 1/2 to 2 hours on about 250° F.

Sneaky Bear Roast

For the non-vegetable eating kids – Scott Young, FL

Bear roast, trim all fat
Large can of mixed vegetables,
    drained

2 large cans of tomato sauce
1 to 2 cups of diced onions

Put 1 can of tomato sauce and mixed vegetables (can use fresh and any type) in the blender, if kids don't like onions then in the blender they go, blend very well till all looks like tomato sauce, pour in crock-pot with other can of tomato sauce mix well, lay in bear roast, season to your taste.

Roasted Leg of Wild Boar

Ryan Simpson, LA

One 6 pound leg of wild boar*
1/4 cup coarse sea salt
1/4 cup coarsely ground black pepper

For the marinade:
4 cups hearty red wine
2 dried imported bay leaves
40 sprigs fresh thyme, rinsed
20 black peppercorns
6 cloves
1 carrot, trimmed, peeled, and cut in 1/4-inch chunks
1 medium onion, cut in eighths
1/4 cup best-quality red wine vinegar

To roast the wild boar:
20 whole cloves
2 to 3 tablespoons olive oil

For the sauce:
2 cups chicken or veal stock
3 tablespoons red current jelly

    1. Rub the leg of wild boar all over with the salt and the pepper. Place it in a shallow dish, cover it loosely, and refrigerate it for 36 hours.

    2. Bring the wine, the herbs and spices, and the vegetables to a boil in a medium-sized saucepan over medium high heat and cook for about 3 minutes. Remove from the heat and let cool to room temperature. Strain, reserving the bay leaf, thyme, peppercorns and cloves, and discarding the vegetables. Whisk in the vinegar.

    3. Quickly rinse the salt and pepper from the boar to remove most but not all of it. Pat meat dry and place it in a shallow dish. Pour the cooled marinade over it, return it to the refrigerator, loosely covered, and let it marinate for 36 hours, turning it at least four times.

    4. Preheat the oven to 450° F.

    5. Remove the leg of wild boar from the marinade and pat it dry. Make 20 tiny slits in it all over, and insert a clove into each slit. Transfer the boar to a baking dish, and pour 1/4 of the marinade over it. Roast in the center of the oven until the boar is very golden on the outside, and when you cut into it is a very faint pink, but not in the least red, which will take about 2 hours. Check it occasionally to be sure the marinade hasn›t completely evaporated, and pour the additional marinade over the roast, 1/4 at a time.

6. When the boar is roasted remove it from the oven, and set it on a platter in warm spot, loosely covered, to sit for at least 20 minutes so the juices have a chance to retreat back into the meat. To prepare the sauce, transfer the cooking juice and any browned bits from the bottom of the baking dish to a medium sized saucepan. Whisk in the chicken or veal stock and bring to a boil over medium-high heat. Reduce by about 1/4, then stir in the red current jelly. Continue cooking and whisking until the sauce is smooth and satiny, 8 to 10 minutes. Remove from the heat.

7. Before slicing the boar remove as many of the cloves as possible. Thinly slice the wild boar and arrange it on a platter. Garnish with flat-leaf parsley leaves. Either pour the sauce over the meat, or serve it on the side.

Hoglicious Ham

Paul Paretta, FL

Green beans
Mojo Corillo dressing

Wild hog ham

In an aluminum foil pan, take ham, fill with Mojo Corillo dressing. Fill up a quarter of the way. Smoke ham for 2 hours. Pour green beans up to cover ham. Seal top with aluminum foil. Check after 5 hours. Yummmmmm.

Venison and Hog Chorizo

Robert Solis, TX

1 pound ground venison
1 pound ground wild hog
1 clove garlic, crushed
1/2 cup ground red pepper
1 teaspoon black pepper
1/4 teaspoon cloves
1/4 teaspoon cinnamon

1/4 teaspoon oregano
1/4 teaspoon cumin
1/4 teaspoon sea salt
1/2 cup apple cider vinegar
2 tablespoons water
10 small hot dried red chile

Mix venison and pork set aside. Combine all other ingredients and mix thoroughly into meat. Cover and refrigerate 24 hours. Divide into 1/4 to 1/2 portions and freeze. To use, crumble and fry in pan combine with eggs may also combine with refried beans or with lightly fried diced potatoes served with a warm soft flour tortilla and picante sauce. You may also add your choice of shredded cheese over taco.

Finger-Licking Squirrel

Jim Horner, KS

5 squirrels, skinned and quartered
1 bottle of barbecue sauce
1 crock-pot

Add squirrel quarters in crock-pot, fill crock-pot half way with water turn on low for 6 hours or till meat falls off bone drain crock-pot and pull off all meat from bone mix meat with barbecue sauce in a bowl and serve on bread. It will melt in your mouth it's that good.

Fried Alligator Nuggets

Joseph Ritchie, MS

Alligator tail
Fish fry
Pepper
Tony's Seasoning
Lemon-pepper seasoning
Cayenne pepper (optional)
Dale's Marinade (low sodium or meat will be too salty)
Cooking Oil

Cut alligator meat off the bone and cut into bite-size nugget pieces. (Make sure you remove all the fat to remove any gamey taste). Marinade in Dale's for 10 minutes. While meat is marinading, prepare fish fry by blending fish fry, pepper, Tony's, lemon-pepper seasoning, and cayanne pepper. (optional). Heat vegetable oil over medium heat. Batter nuggets with fish fry seasoning blend. Fry in vegetable oil till nuggets float or till golden brown. Enjoy!!